**Analytical Methods in Loan
Evaluation**

Analytical Methods in Loan Evaluation

Yair E. Orgler
Tel-Aviv University

Lexington Books
D.C. Heath and Company
Lexington, Massachusetts
Toronto   London

"A Credit Scoring Model for Commercial Loans" is reprinted, with revisions, from the *Journal of Money, Credit, and Banking,* Volume 2 (November 1970), pp. 435-45. Copyright © 1970 by the Ohio State University Press.

Library of Congress Cataloging in Publication Data

Orgler, Yair E
 Analytical methods in loan evaluation.

 Bibliography: p. 107.
 Includes index.
 1. Bank loans. 2. Bank loans—Mathematical models. I. Title.
HG1641.074 332.1'753'0151 74-15536
ISBN 0-669-96065-9

Published simultaneously in Canada

Printed in the United States of America

International Standard Book Number: 0-669-96065-9

Library of Congress Catalog Card Number: 74-15536

To My Wife

Contents

viii

List of Figures

List of Tables

Foreword

In recent years, the scope and magnitude of bank operations have expanded greatly. These developments have been accompanied by an increased willingness on the part of bankers to accept risk at the same time that changes in the economy and financial markets, both in the U.S. and abroad, have put added strains on the safety and soundness we have come to expect from our banking system. The job of those who are responsible for evaluating the degree of risk in the financial institutions' asset portfolios has become more difficult and more critical. This applies both to the staff of the institutions themselves and to those outside, such as auditors and government agency examiners.

It has been increasingly difficult for the Federal Deposit Insurance Corporation and the other supervisory agencies to expand their trained examining forces sufficiently to keep pace with developments in the industry. Under the last two Chairmen of the Federal Deposit Insurance Corporation, K. A. Randall and Frank Wille, a concerted effort has been made to apply quantitative techniques to the problems of bank supervision. This book presents the results of research aimed at the problems in one most important area—loan evaluation.

Successful application of management science techniques to new areas is a rather slow process. It requires not only selection of the appropriate analytical method, but the careful consideration of all the real world complications. Equally as important as the technical problem-solving aspect is the need to communicate the technique to the practitioner who must be persuaded to change his established methods. I believe that Dr. Orgler's work is an important step both in problem solving and in communication. I am confident that publication of these studies will assist in increasing application of these techniques and in encouraging further research in this area.

Paul M. Horvitz
Director of Research
Federal Deposit Insurance Corporation

Preface

In recent years, an increasing number of management science models in banking have been derived and implemented. Surprisingly enough, only a relatively small portion of these applications are related to loan evaluation, which is one of the most important and difficult tasks in credit management by banks and other lending institutions.

This manuscript presents new developments in the application of quantitative techniques to loan evaluation and review. Hence, this book is equally relevant to bank loan officers, credit managers of other lending institutions, examiners of bank regulatory agencies, bank auditors, and students of financial institutions.

Except for Chapter 3, which is a survey article on credit-scoring methods, the studies represent original work performed by the author while he was working as a financial economist with the Research Division of the Federal Deposit Insurance Corporation (FDIC). The studies cover two major areas: loan selection and loan analysis. The first subject includes an empirical study of the common cutoff selection procedure and a normative model designed to perform the same task in a more efficient way. The second subject contains three studies: two general credit-scoring models for evaluating outstanding commercial and consumer loans, and one special-purpose model designed for estimating the potential losses from an entire consumer loans portfolio held by a defaulted bank.

The methodology used in the different studies varies according to the subject that is covered: linear programming is used in developing the loan selection model; multivariate regression analysis is the underlying statistical technique in deriving the credit-scoring models; and a Markov chains process provides the basis for calculating the loss potential of a consumer loans portfolio. While each of these techniques is quite complex, the book emphasizes their applicability to the problems discussed and not their mathematical and statistical properties.

Several of the enclosed studies were published in abridged form in the financial literature. The book includes some of the material that was omitted from earlier publications because of space limitations. Moreover, all the material has been revised substantially and edited to form a homogeneous manuscript.

This manuscript could not have been written without the support of the FDIC and without the help, advice, and encouragement of Paul Horvitz, the FDIC director of research. Helpful comments were also made by Robert Eisenbeis and Panos Konstas of the FDIC, Neil Murphy of the University of Maine, and Benjamin Wolkowitz of the Federal Reserve Board. The final draft of the manuscript was written while the author was a visiting professor with the Board of Governors of the Federal Reserve System. The views expressed in this book are those of the author and not necessarily those of the FDIC and/or the Federal Reserve Board.

Introduction

Since the early 1960s, an increasing number of management science applications to banking have been developed.[a] Implementation of these methods was slow in the early stages but has gained momentum in recent years. The level of model sophistication and the success in implementation vary, depending largely on the banking activity for which a model has been developed. The models that have been applied successfully cover a variety of areas, such as bank operations, the trust department, the bond department, and general management aids.

One of the areas that has received relatively little attention is the loan function. A survey of management science projects in banking, conducted by Bank Administration Institute, shows that the total number of projects in the commercial loan area reported by forty-one banks was seventy-seven, of which forty-two were completed and partially or fully implemented (twenty-one projects were in progress and fourteen were planned to begin within a year).[b] Parallel figures for installment credit were twenty-five projects implemented out of sixty-one. In contrast, fifty-seven out of 167 projects were implemented in the trust department, ninety-five out of 216 in bank operations, and 175 out of 415 in general management aids. The relatively small number of management science projects in the commercial and consumer loan fields is quite surprising since the loan function is one of the most important areas of bank activity. It may only be explained by the difficulties involved in developing analytical methods for loan management.

The purpose of this manuscript is to present several analytical studies in loan evaluation. The emphasis in these studies is on the review and examination of existing loans. The loan review process is comparable to both quality control and research and development in industry,[c] while loan examination is one of the most important activities of bank examiners. Both loan review and loan examination have received little attention in the literature, and no analytical

---

[a]For a collection of studies on this subject, see Cohen and Hammer [16], Jessup [38, part 5], and Eilon and Fowkes [23]. More recent readings can be found primarily in the *Journal of Financial and Quantitative Analysis* and the *Journal of Bank Research*.

[b]The survey results are summarized by Williams [60].

[c]For a detailed analysis of this comparison, together with a description of a successful loan review process, see Sax [57].

models have been developed in these areas. The studies contained in this manuscript are designed to close this gap and to provide loan review officers and bank examiners with efficient analytical tools. It should be emphasized that the models developed in these studies are complements to, rather than substitutes for, human judgment and experience.

Scope of the Studies

When an outstanding loan portfolio has to be reviewed or examined, the first problem is to determine which loans are to be evaluated, since evaluating every loan is impractical and often unfeasible. Hence, loan evaluation can be divided into two phases: (1) selecting loans for analysis and (2) analyzing the selected loans. The first two chapters cover the first phase and the remaining four chapters are devoted to the second phase.

There are few formal procedures for selecting loans for evaluation. Large commercial banks often review their existing loans on a continuous basis or concentrate on special types of loans that are potentially more risky, for instance, loans with a poor payment performance. On the other hand, bank examiners use a well-defined method for selecting loans for examination. They define a dollar cutoff level and examine all the loans with balances higher than this level (they also examine certain loans with lower balances). Chapter 1 contains an empirical analysis of the cutoff selection method and points out the disadvantages of this approach. It also presents alternative approaches to the loan selection problem.

One of the alternative approaches to the cutoff selection method is to determine the optimal coverage of each loan category so that the total review time (or cost) is minimized or that the quality of coverage, subject to time constraints, is maximized. A linear programming model that provides these results is presented in Chapter 2. Several versions of the model are developed and illustrated with a numerical example. The model is then tested with data obtained from routine examinations of fifty commercial banks. The outcome of these tests indicates that use of the model will result either in time saving or in improving the quality of evaluation and possibly in both. Because of its simplicity and generality, the model can be adapted to the needs of different banking institutions.

The second and more difficult phase of evaluation begins once a sufficient number of loans has been selected. While the experience and the judgment of loan review officers and bank examiners have always played major roles in loan evaluation, new analytical methods provide important aids in performing this task. In screening consumer loan applications, the best known analytical tool is credit scoring. It provides a formula that determines whether to accept, reject, or further analyze a loan application. Thus, the limited time of experienced loan officers is efficiently allocated only to marginal cases.

Credit scoring models are not limited to screening new loan applications. They can be used for evaluating existing loans and for a variety of other applications. Consequently, we provide in Chapter 3 a detailed discussion of the concepts, principles, and procedures involved in developing and implementing a credit-scoring model. The chapter also lists a large number of different applications of this method and describes the favorable experience of banks and other financial institutions that have used credit-scoring models in recent years.

Two specific applications of the credit-scoring method to loan evaluation are presented in Chapters 4 and 5. Chapter 4 presents a model for evaluating existing commercial loans. Multivariate regression analysis is used to derive the credit-scoring function, which contains several somewhat unusual independent variables; for example, dummy variables are used to indicate whether a loan is secured or unsecured and whether a borrower's statements were audited or not. Analysis of the regression results and a comparison of model predictions with actual loan classifications demonstrate the applicability of this model to the review and examination of commercial loans.

Chapter 5 presents three credit-scoring models for evaluating outstanding consumer loans. The models were developed for two commercial banks: two models are designed for periodic reviews by each of the two banks while the third applies to both banks and represents an attempt to develop a more general model that could be used for loan evaluations by bank examiners. The results show that the variables providing the best discrimination between good and bad loans are based on loan repayment information. Since these variables were not the same for both banks, they were not included in the combined model. Consequently, the classification results for the individual models are better than those obtained for the joint model.

Chapter 6 describes an alternative approach to scoring individual loans. The analytical method suggested for this approach is based on a Markov chains process. Unlike the previous studies, which contain models designed for a wide range of applications, the objective of this study is to solve a specific problem that the FDIC has encountered and that could not be solved in a conventional way. The problem involved the estimation of potential losses from a large consumer loans portfolio held by a defaulted bank. The solution provided by the model has resulted in substantial savings to the FDIC. Although the estimation method presented in Chapter 6 was designed for a specific case, a modified procedure may be useful in similar situations, such as, when the potential loss from an entire consumer loans portfolio must be estimated for acquisition, investment, or special examination purposes.

1 Selection of Bank Loans for Evaluation

Among the many responsibilities of bank management and bank regulatory agencies, the periodic review of bank loan portfolios stands out in its importance and complexity. In recent years, the proportion of loans to total assets has been well over 50 percent, and in many banks this percentage is much higher.[a] The importance of proper management and evaluation of this major bank asset is compounded by the fact that loans genrally are more risky than any other earning asset. Inadequate management of the loan portfolio may even cause a bank to default, as evidenced by seven out of fifty-four recent bank failures.[b]

The loan review function is comparable to quality control in industry, and it can also perform the research and development function in bank lending.[c] In one bank, the loan review department has helped to reduce the net loan charge-offs from 1.02 percent of average loans outstanding in 1965 to 0.10 percent in 1971, while the loan portfolio continued to grow rapidly. In addition, the loan review department has developed systematic means of exploring new lending techniques. While this may represent an unusually successful case, the important and active role of the loan review function in bank loan management is recognized in many articles on this subject (for example, see the articles by Burnham [13] and Hoskin [34]). In practice, however, an independent loan review function is normally limited to large banks. It is not surprising, therefore, that inadequate loan supervision is considered one of the basic causes of potential loan problems (see Jacobsen [37,p. 49] and the FDIC Manual of Examination Policies [45, p. 3]).

Another aspect of the loan review function is the resemblence

---

[a]The proportion of loans and discounts to total assets of all insured commercial banks was 55.7 percent on 31 December 1973 [7].

[b]The other failures are attributed to self-serving loans, embezzlements, and misuse of brokered funds. For details about these cases, see Barnett [8]. A detailed analysis of bank failures over a longer period appears in Benston [11].

[c]A detailed analysis of this comparison and a description of a successful loan review department appears in a paper by Sax [57].

between loan review and loan examination by bank regulatory agencies. In some banks, the loan review department serves as liaison between the bank and the examiners. Moreover, the function and even the attitude of internal loan review officers in many large banks is similar to that of bank examiners.[d]

An excellent description of the loan review function and its relationship to loan examination is provided by Crosse:

More importantly, the affairs of borrowers having outstanding loans need careful periodic review and reevaluation. It is the responsibility of the credit review function to point out any signs of developing weakness in a borrower's affairs and to warn of danger before the bank is faced with a salvage situation. Few loans are bad when made, but even good credits can deteriorate. Careful watching alone can spare a bank from unnecessary losses.

Bank examiners and outside accountants (if requested) perform a somewhat similar function. Their review and classification of outstanding loans is, in effect, an objective credit analysis designed to point out weaknesses of which the directors and senior management should be cognizant. Their periodic visits, however, may be too infrequent to provide timely warnings. Moreover, their analyses can be based solely on the information available in the credit files or on the lending officers' specific knowledge. Examination is not a substitute for a continuing credit review within the bank itself. At best it serves as a check or audit of the credit review process.

Recognizing the value of such a check, some of the largest banks, in recent years, have established loan review sections whose sole function is to conduct a continuous review of outstanding loans from what is essentially the bank examiner's point of view. In effect, this is an audit review of the work of both the lending officers and the credit department.[e]

Although bank executives realize the importance of evaluating outstanding loans, there are few formal methods for dealing with the loan review function. Some large banks have established loan review departments whose function is to evaluate existing loans in a routine and systematic manner, while other banks conduct periodic reviews of randomly selected loans.

Complete coverage of all loans during a periodic review or examination is both impossible and unnecessary; hence, a certain portion of the loan portfolio has to be selected for evaluation. This

---

[d]A statement to this effect was made by Phalen [40, p.51] in a recent panel discussion on new trends in lending.

[e]Howard D. Crosse [17, p. 214].

selection process is most important since it affects the conclusions drawn on the entire loan portfolio. The purpose of this chapter is to present and analyze a common loan selection procedure and to discuss alternative approaches to the selection problem.

The Cutoff Method[f]

Bank regulatory agencies use a well-defined method for selecting bank loans for examination. Because of its widespread use, the examiners' loan selection procedure is analyzed in detail in this section.

Bank examiners define a cutoff level in terms of dollars and evaluate every loan whose outstanding balance exceeds this level. Past due loans and loans that have been previously scheduled are also examined, even if their current balance is below the cutoff level.[g] In addition, some examiners use judgmental sampling in selecting for evaluation a random sample of loans with smaller balances (see Jacobs [36, pp. 2-3]).

The cutoff selection procedure does not provide information on the bulk of smaller loans, on the performance of loan officers who concentrate on the evaluation of small loans, or on the loan port-folios of some small branches. The neglect of small loans is ex-plained by the lack of immediate danger to depositors' funds from the default of such loans. This approach may satisfy the short-run objective of loan evaluations, but it is inadequate for long-run goals. As demonstrated by the failure of Public Bank of Detroit, even a consumer loan portfolio may lead to a bank's default in the long run if the loans are badly managed and if a sizable share of total loans belongs to this category. Public Bank was one of the largest banks that ever failed, and its failure was primarily attributed to poor

[f]A small portion of this section appears in an earlier paper "Selection of Bank Loans for Evaluation: An Analytical Approach," in the *Journal of Finance* [51].

[g]Previously scheduled loans include loans that in the last examination were either classified, listed for special mention, or listed for technical exceptions. According to the FDIC Manual of Examination Policies [45], loan classifications "...are expressions of different degrees of a common factor—risk of non-payment" (p.4); loans listed for special mention "...are loans which do not presently expose the bank to a sufficient degree of risk to warrant adverse classification, but which possess credit deficiencies deserving management's close attention" (p. 5); and loans listed for technical exceptions involve technical deficiencies in documenta-tion that "...should be brought to the attention of management for remedial action" (p. 7). Any loan which, according to the judgment of an examiner, belongs to one of these categories is listed in the report of examination.

management of home improvement loans (see Chapter 6). At the time of insolvency, consumer loans amounted to 52.7 percent of total loans. Fourteen months later this proportion increased to 67.6 percent because the collection of consumer loans was slower than for any other type of loan. Moreover, the highest losses were incurred in this category.

Another major problem associated with the cutoff method is the determination of the cutoff level itself. In most cases, this level is left to the judgment of the examiner in the field. According to Hall [30, p. 26], the cutoff level is primarily determined on the basis of a bank's size and capital structure. Other variables that are relevant in determining a cutoff level are mentioned by Roberts [56, pp. 24-25]. They include, among others, the volume of loans classified at the previous examination, the ratio of total capital to total assets, the change in this proportion since the last examination, and the quality of management.

A cross-section analysis was undertaken to try to identify the factors that affect the determination of loan selection cutoff levels. An initial review of several hundred FDIC examination reports showed a strong relationship between successive cutoff levels for the same bank. In many cases, a bank's cutoff level remained constant for several years, despite changes in the size of the bank and in the quality of its loan portfolio. These observations led us to the hypothesis that the main factor in selecting a cutoff level for a certain examination is the cutoff point used in the previous examination of the same bank. Some correlation between cutoff levels and capital accounts was also expected since this relationship was explicitly established by some examiners. Also to be determined was whether other relevant elements are considered systematically and whether they have a significant influence on the definition of loan cutoff levels. A multivariate regression analysis was used to test our basic hypothesis and some of the related questions.

The dependent, or explained, variable is the cutoff point used in the current examination of each bank in the sample. The independent, or explaining, variables cover a variety of elements, all of which are considered to be relevant to the definition of the cutoff level. These variables are chosen not only because of their possible effect on the cutoff level but also because they are readily available to the examiner at the early stages of an examination. They are all

Table 1-1

Notation for Cross-Section Analysis of Loan Examination Cutoff Levels

Description	Notation
1. Cutoff level—current examination (t)	min_t
2. Cutoff level—previous examination $(t-1)$	min_{t-1}
3. Net operating earnings divided by average assets $(t-1)$	E_{t-1}
4. Overdue loans divided by total loans $(t-1)$	PD_{t-1}
5. Total assets (t)	TA_t
6. Common stock plus surplus (t)	CS_t
7. Total classified loans $(t-1)$	CL_{t-1}
8. Total loans (gross) $(t-1)$	TL_{t-1}
9. Classification ratio (CL_{t-1}/TL_{t-1})	R_1
10. Previous classification ratio (CL_{t-2}/TL_{t-2})	R_2
11. Change in classification ratio (R_1/R_2)	R
12. Total capital accounts (t)	CA_t

based on the underlying variables listed in Table 1-1. Some of the independent variables in the regression program are the same as the underlying elements in Table 1-1; others represent a simple function of one or two of these items.

A sample of 100 nonmember commercial banks from four FDIC regions was selected for the analysis. The data from three consecutive examinations of these banks were obtained from FDIC examination reports. The variables that were incorporated in the cross-section analysis are listed in Table 1-2.

The results of the analysis confirm our basic assumption about the effect of the previous cutoff level, and the widespread practice of defining min_t as a percentage of common stock plus surplus (see Table 1-2). The results also indicate that all other potentially relevant elements did not have a significant effect on the selection of the cutoff level.

Additional regression tests with various combinations of the explaining variables give the same results. The only consistently significant variables are the previous cutoff level (min_{t-1}) and common stock plus surplus (CS_t). In all these cases, the previous cutoff level explains most of the variation in the dependent variable. In a simple regression the previous cutoff level (min_{t-1}) by itself accounts

Table 1-2

Regression Results of Cross-Section Analysis of Loan Examination Cutoff Levels

Variable	Coefficient	Standard Error	t Value[a]
1. min_{t-1}	0.913	0.073	12.491[b]
2. E_{t-1}	0.134	0.348	0.384
3. PD_{t-1}	0.092	0.081	1.137
4. TA_t/TA_{t-1}	−0.092	1.459	−0.063
5. $CS_t \times 10^{-3}$	0.306	0.140	2.187[c]
6. R_1	−1.686	6.938	−0.243
7. R_2	3.156	5.773	0.547
8. R	−0.003	0.003	−1.087
9. PD_{t-1}/PD_{t-2}	−0.076	0.133	−0.575
10. E_{t-1}/E_{t-2}	−0.019	0.020	−0.956
11. TL_t/TL_{t-1}	1.805	1.181	1.528
12. CA_t/TA_t	4.105	7.183	0.572
13. CA_{t-1}/CL_{t-1}	−0.001	0.001	−0.780
14. TL_t/TA_t	−2.209	1.673	−1.320

$R^2 = 0.803$;
adjusted $R^2 = 0.773$;
intercept $= -1.061$;
observations $= 100$.

[a]Because of rounding, t is not exactly equal to the ratio: coefficient/standard error.
[b]Significant at the 1 percent level.
[c]Significant at the 5 percent level.

for 77 percent of the variation in the current cutoff point (min_t). A similar run with common stock plus surplus (CS_t) accounts for only 32 percent of the same variation.[h]

Alternative Approaches

The deficiencies of the cutoff procedure suggest that different approaches to the problem of loan selection are desirable. Moreover, the complexity of the problem and the measurability of many of its relevent factors point to the possibility of obtaining an analytical solution. There are several alternative methods for solving the loan selection problem; all are based on quantitative techniques.

[h]It is interesting to note that the regression coefficient of CS_t when used alone was 0.012. This coefficient is close to the 1 percent factor that is often used by FDIC examiners.

The first alternative is to reformulate the current procedure so that it explicitly takes into account the quality, diversification, and size of the loan portfolio in defining the cutoff level. This approach is rejected because of the difficulty in establishing criteria for judging the adequacy of a cutoff level. Moreover, any selection procedure that is based on a cutoff level ignores all the loans with smaller balances.

A second analytical method is based on a stratified statistical sampling program. This approach provides adequate coverage for small loans, but it has its own disadvantages. The variety in loan types, with respect to size, collateral, type of borrower, and so on, may cause some difficulties when statistical sampling is used, especially in the case of commercial loans. For an effective selection procedure, the loan portfolio has to be divided into a large number of homogeneous but relatively small strata, where statistical sampling becomes inefficient, and the total size of combined samples may result in time requirements and expenses in excess of available resources.

A third alternative is a combination of the first two methods. It is based on a relatively high cutoff level plus a statistical sampling procedure for all loans with balances smaller than the cutoff. This method represents a stratified sampling program where two strata are defined by a subjective cutoff level: one stratum contains all the large loans and is completely covered, while a second stratum of smaller loans is randomly sampled. Although this method is an improvement of the current cutoff procedure, it suffers from the combined disadvantages of the two previous alternatives: first, it is based on a subjective cutoff level, and, second, if the cutoff is relatively high, most of the loans will be subject to sampling— presenting the same difficulties associated with sampling the entire loan portfolio.

A fourth approach to the loan selection problem is based on a linear programming model. A model of this type may minimize the loan evaluation time subject to coverage constraints or maximize the quality of coverage subject to time constraints. Other goals or objective functions can be used, and additional constraints can be imposed. The main advantage of the linear programming model lies in its explicit and simultaneous control over time, coverage, and other relevant aspects of loan selection. A model of this type can be easily solved on a computer. It can also be subjected to sensitivity analysis to provide useful information about the parameters with the largest influence on the optimal results. The following chapter presents a linear programming model for loan selection.

2

A Linear Programming
Model for Loan Selection

Linear programming is a technique that maximizes or minimizes a linear objective function subject to a set of linear constraints. Problems solved with linear programming belong to a broad class of allocation problems that arise when a number of tasks have to be performed subject to a variety of constraints on resources. Because of these limitations, it is impossible to allocate available resources so that each activity will be executed. Instead, the limited resources are allocated in such a way that the effectiveness of the whole process is maximized. One of the relatively simple allocation problems involves a linear decision function and linear constraints, and it is solved by linear programming. The loan selection problem appears to fit into this category.

The Model

The loan selection model can be formulated in two different ways: (1) minimization of the cost or time of loan evaluation subject to coverage and quality constraints; or (2) maximization of coverage or quality subject to time or cost constraints. In both cases, the decision variables represent the amount and/or number of loans to be evaluated in each predetermined loan category.

The definition of loan categories depends on the task that is to be performed—that is, internal review or external examination. Thus, some banks may subdivide their loan portfolio according to their branches for branch performance comparisons or according to individual loan officers for control and supervision purposes. Regulatory agencies are more limited in their choice; they must define their decision variables according to the existing distribution of loan files in each examined bank—for example, by economic sector or by collateral.

A small portion of this chapter appears in an earlier paper: "Selection of Bank Loans for Evaluation: An Analytical Approach," in the *Journal of Finance* [51].

In this model, the loan portfolio is separated into commercial, real estate, and consumer loans.[a] These segregations were chosen because of the differences in the characteristics and qualities of loans in the three categories.[b] Finer breakdowns are, of course, desirable; but the selected breakdown is adequate for illustrative purposes, and it may be useful for actual implementation, especially in small and medium-size banks.

The separation of loans into three categories means that the linear programming model incorporates three decision variables. A more detailed breakdown of the loan portfolio results in additional decision variables, but the basic development of the model remains the same. Let X_i represent the amount of loans to be reviewed in the ith category, where $i=1$ refers to commercial loans, $i=2$ represents real estate loans, and $i=3$ refers to consumer loans. Similarly, let x_i represent the number of loans[c] to be reviewed in the ith category, where $i=1, 2, 3$. Most of the remaining notation appears in Appendix 2A. (This is a sample of the form used in the loan examination survey that provided the data for testing the model). In general, capital letters represent dollar values and lower-case letters refer to numbers.

Since it is possible to derive different versions of the model for different institutions and different loan selection objectives, no particular model is recommended. Instead, several alternative formats are presented. The models are formulated in the most simple way, both for illustrative purposes and for wide-scale implementation.

Version 1

The objective of the first version of the model is to minimize the evaluation time subject to coverage constraints. Let D_i express the minimal fraction of loans in category i that should be evaluated, and

---

[a] Consumer loans are often referred to as installment loans because most consumer loans are paid in installments. In this book, the terms consumer loans and installment loans are used interchangeably.

[b] A brief analysis of the data collected for testing the model (see the section on "Testing the Model" later in this chapter) indicates that there are substantial differences in the classification ratios of the three loan categories.

[c] When the model is solved for the number of loans to be reviewed, all loans to a single borrower are normally combined into one "line." The model can also be solved for individual loans if this is more desirable.

let D represent the minimal fraction of the total amount of loans that must be reviewed. L_i is the balance of loans in category i (in thousands of dollars) and T_i is the average evaluation time per \$1000 (see Appendix 2A).[d] Given this notation, the first version of the model has the *objective function*[e]

$$\min Z = \sum_{i=1}^{3} T_i X_i, \tag{2.1}$$

which is subject to the *constraints*

$$X_i \le L_i, \quad \text{for } i=1, 2, 3 , \tag{2.2}$$

$$X_i \ge D_i L_i , \quad \text{for } i=1, 2, 3 , \tag{2.3}$$

$$\sum_{i=1}^{3} X_i \ge DL, \quad \text{where } L = \sum_{i=1}^{3} L_i. \tag{2.4}$$

The first type of constraint [Equation (2.2)] is required because of the structure of linear programming models. It simply imposes an upper limit on the amount that can be examined in each loan category. The remaining constraints impose subjective coverage requirements on each loan category and on the entire portfolio. Since the subjective nature of the cutoff level has been criticized in the previous chapter, it is necessary to explain the use of subjective coverage constraints: first, unlike the single cutoff point, different coverage requirements are imposed on different types of loans and on the entire portfolio. Second, coverage requirements are more meaningful than a cutoff level since the actual objective of many examiners is to review a given proportion of the portfolio rather than examine loans above a certain size. Finally, the coverage constraints can be evaluated with the dual variables (shadow prices) that are an integral part of the solution. The dual values indicate the

[d]The equation $T_i = 60h_i/E_i$ is used to obtain approximate time estimates for testing purposes. For actual implementation, a more accurate procedure for estimating evaluation times should be used.

[e]It should be noted that this simple version can be solved without a linear programming algorithm. First, the coverage constraints in each category have to be satisfied. Then, the total coverage constraint has to be met by selecting loans from the category with the lowest T_i without violating the first set of constraints ($X_i \le L_i$). A simple solution of this kind will be infeasible in an actual loan selection model, which will contain additional and more complicated constraints.

precise impact of each constraint on the optimal solution.[f] Thus, the dual of a coverage constraint is equal to the expected change in optimal evaluation time resulting from a change in coverage requirements. Given this information, the coverage constraint may be revised.

The first version of the model can also be solved for the number of loans to be examined (x_i). To obtain this solution, it is necessary to replace T_i by t_i, D_i by d_i, and L_i by n_i.

Version 2

The objective of the second version is to concentrate the evaluation effort on loan categories with the highest loss potential. This objective is achieved by maximizing the expected value of classified loans, where P_i is the classification ratio per \$1000 worth of loans in category i. This version is subject to a time constraint, where T is the overall time allocated for loan evaluation, and to the same coverage constraints that are imposed on the first version. For this version, the *objective function* is

$$\max \quad Y = \sum_{i=1}^{3} P_i X_i \tag{2.5}$$

subject to the *constraints*

$$\sum_{i=1}^{3} T_i X_i \leq T , \tag{2.6}$$

$$X_i \leq L_i , \text{ for } i=1, 2, 3 , \tag{2.7}$$

$$X_i \geq D_i L_i , \text{ for } i=1, 2, 3 , \tag{2.8}$$

$$\sum_{i=1}^{3} X_i \geq DL . \tag{2.9}$$

The overall time limit (T) can be based on manpower availability, on time spent in previous reviews, or on the subjective decision of a bank officer, examiner, or auditor. It should be noted that the

---

[f] When the dual variable is equal to zero, the constraint is not binding and has no impact on the outcome.

estimation of T_i and P_i is quite difficult. Nevertheless, as long as these parameters are estimated in the same way for all categories, the optimal time allocation among the categories will not be affected even if the estimates are not very accurate.

Version 3

The third version of the model is the same as the second one, except for the objective function, which simply maximizes the amount of coverage, and the last constraint, which is omitted:

$$\max \quad W = \sum_{i=1}^{3} X_i . \tag{2.10}$$

This version is inferior to the second model because it does not consider the qualities of the loans in the different categories; therefore, the use of this objective function is not recommended. It is included only because it appears to represent the goal pursued by some examiners when they select loans for evaluation.

Combined Versions

Another possibility is to combine the first two versions in a two-stage process where the optimal value of the objective function obtained from Version 1 (minimal evaluation time) is substituted for the total available time (T) in the first constraint of Version 2. As a result, the minimal amount of examination time is allocated to the n loan categories according to their quality as measured by the classification rate (P_i). In this process, the coverage requirements (D_i and especially D) in the second version may have to be reduced in order to obtain an allocation different from the first version.

Additional versions can be easily developed in a similar way. These models may vary from the given examples in objective functions, in constraints, and in decision variables. The number of loan categories, and consequently the number of decision variables, is unlimited for any practical application of the model. Moreover, loans can be divided according to two characteristics, say, by type and by size. In this case, decision variables with two indices may be used. For example, X_{ij} may represent the amount of loans of the ith type and the jth size category.

Numerical Example

This section presents a numerical example that illustrates how the model is applied to an actual case. The data are from one of the banks for which information was obtained in the loan examination survey (the figures are listed in Appendix 2B). With the exception of coverage requirements, all the parameters in the example are based on these data. For instance, $T_i = 60h_i/E_i = (60) (65)/3765 = 1.04$ minutes per \$1000 of commercial loans.[g]

The selected coverage requirements are 60 percent for total loans, 50 percent for commercial loans, 20 percent for real estate loans, and 10 percent for consumer loans. The overall coverage of 60 percent corresponds to the 63 percent actual coverage of all the banks in the survey. This means that the model provides nearly the same overall coverage of the loan portfolio as an average bank in the survey. On the other hand, minimal coverage requirements for each type of loan are lower than the actual fractions, especially for real estate loans. The lower coverage requirements allow more flexibility in allocating evaluation time while maintaining minimal coverages. The value of D_2 (20 percent) was deliberately set at a much lower level than the actual rate (66 percent) since the low classification ratio in the real estate category did not seem to justify such a high coverage.

Substituting the coverage requirements and the calculated values of the parameters into Equations (2.1)-(2.4), we obtain the *objective function* given by Version 1 of the model for the selected bank

$$\text{min. } Z = 1.04X_1 + 3.35X_2 + 6.1X_3,$$

subject to the following *constraints* (all figures are in thousands of dollars):

[g]For comparative reasons, all the parameters are based on the same examination for which the model is solved. In practical implementations, these parameters will be based on previous examinations and on additional information. More details about implementing the loan selection model appear in the section on "Implementation" later in this chapter.

$$X_1 \leq 4365,$$
$$X_2 \leq 680,$$
$$X_3 \leq 778,$$
$$X_1 \geq 2182.5,$$
$$X_2 \geq 136,$$
$$X_3 \geq 77.8,$$
$$X_1 + X_2 + X_3 \geq 3493.8.$$

Although this simple case can be solved manually, it was solved on a computer terminal (see Appendix 2C). The results are listed in Table 2-1 in comparison with the actual loan evaluation. The results indicate a time saving of 32 percent. This reduction is obtained from lower coverages, especially in the real estate category. The resulting coverages are 60 percent for total loans, and 75, 20, and 10 percent for commercial, real estate, and installment loans, respectively.

The model also provides a list of dual variables that evaluate the effect of each constraint on the results (see the entries at the bottom of Appendix 2C). For example, the dual variable of column 5 evaluates the change in optimal evaluation time due to a change in the coverage requirement for real estate loans. The value of this dual variable is 2.31, which means that a $1000 increase in coverage of real estate loans will require 2.31 more minutes. This increase is less than the average evaluation time for real estate loans, which is equal to 3.35 minutes per $1000. The difference is explained by the fact that an increased coverage in the real estate category is partially offset by a reduction of coverage in the commercial category, since the total coverage requirement has not been changed. Hence, the net change in examination time is equal to $T_2 - T_1 = 3.35 - 1.04 = 2.31$. It is apparent, therefore, that a change in one constraint may affect several decision variables and that the dual model takes these joint effects into consideration.

The dual variables can be obtained both in absolute terms (minutes per $1000 of loans) and in relative terms (minutes per 1 percent of coverage), the latter requiring a slight modification in the structure of the model. For example, the second coverage constraint, which is $X_2 \geq (0.2)(680)$, becomes $100X_2/680 \geq 20$ or $0.147X_2 \geq 20$, where the right-hand-side element represents the 20 percent cover-

Table 2-1

Model Results Compared to Actual Evaluation: Version 1 —Numerical Example

	Model	Actual evaluation	Difference Amount	Difference Percentage[a]
Time (in minutes)	4341	6360	−2019	−32
Loans evaluated (in thousands of dollars)				
Commercial	3280	3765	−485	−13
Real estate	136	627	−491	−78
Consumer	78	59	19	32
Total	3494	4451	−957	−21
Loan coverage (in percent)				
Commercial	75	86	−11	
Real estate	20	92	−72	
Consumer	10	8	2	
Total	60	76	−16	

[a]The difference as a percentage of actual evaluation figures.

age requirement. The dual variable of this constraint is equal to 15.7, which means that a 1 percent increase in the coverage of real estate loans will require 15.7 more minutes for loan evaluations. This result applies to a marginal change of 1 percent, but it is likely to be the same for a wider range. Existing computer programs provide information not only about marginal changes in the parameters but also about the range for which these changes hold. An extension of the dual value over its valid range may indicate, for example, that a 15 percent increase in coverage of real estate loans will require about four more hours.

In Version 2 of the model, the objective function maximizes the expected value of classified loans, subject to a time constraint and exactly the same coverage constraints used in the first version. All the parameters remain unchanged and only three new coefficients (P_1, P_2, P_3) are computed from the data in Appendix 2B. Substituting P_i into Equations (2.5)-(2.9), we obtain the *objective function*

$$\text{max. } Y = 0.097X_1 + 0.018X_2 + 0X_3,$$

Subject to the *constraints*

$$1.04X_1 + 3.35X_2 + 6.1X_3 \leq 6360,$$

$$X_1 \leq 4365,$$

$$X_2 \leq 680,$$

$$X_3 \leq 778,$$

$$X_1 \geq 2182.5,$$

$$X_2 \geq 136,$$

$$X_3 \geq 77.8,$$

$$X_1 + X_2 + X_3 \geq 3493.8.$$

The results of this example show an increase of 14 percent in the expected amount of classified loans together with increased coverages in the commercial and consumer loans categories. This improvement is obtained with the same amount of time that was spent in the actual evaluation by redistributing the selected loans. (Table 2-2 lists the results of Version 2 of the model in comparison to actual evaluation data).

Testing the Model

The purpose of this section is to test the model with actual data provided by FDIC examiners for fifty banks from twelve states (see Table 2-3). The data were obtained during routine examinations of randomly selected banks and were reported on a special form (see Appendix 2D).

The model is tested by solving both Versions 1 and 2 for each of the fifty banks. Each case is solved in the same way as the numerical example and with identical coverage requirements: 60 percent for the entire loan portfolio and 50, 20, and 10 percent for commercial, real estate, and consumer loans, respectively. The use of a single set of coverage requirements for banks that differ substantially in geographical location and size does not provide the best possible results but is necessary for comparative purposes.

As shown in Table 2-4, the solution of the first version results in an overall time saving of 10.3 percent for all fifty banks. Thirteen of

Table 2-2

Model Results Compared to Actual Evaluation: Version 2 —Numerical Example

	Model	Actual evaluation	Difference Amount	Difference Percentage[a]
Classified loans (in thousands of dollars)	431	378	53	14
Loans examined (in thousands of dollars)				
Commercial	4365	3765	600	16
Real estate	402	627	−225	−36
Consumer	78	59	19	32
Total	4845	4451	394	9
Loan coverage (in percent)				
Commercial	100	86	14	
Real estate	59	92	−33	
Consumer	10	8	2	
Total	83	76	7	

[a]The difference as a percentage of actual evaluation figures.

Table 2-3

Distribution by Total Assets of Fifty Banks from Twelve States

Total assets	Number of banks
Less than $ 2,000,000	10
$ 2,000,000-$ 5,000,000	19
$ 5,000,000-$10,000,000	13
$10,000,000-$25,000,000	8
Total	50

these banks require more time than was actually spent during the examination process. The remaining thirty-seven cases show a time saving of 23.8 percent. Individual results vary substantially because of the uniform reserve requirements and the differences among the banks. Time savings range between 1 percent and 44 percent, although one case requires as much as 232 percent more time in the loan selection model than was actually spent during the examination.

Table 2-4

Model Results Compared to Actual Evaluations: Version 1—Fifty Banks

	Model	Actual evaluation[a]	Difference	
			Amount	Percentage[b]
Thirty-seven banks (demonstrated time savings)				
Total time (in hours)	1,572	2,062	−490	−23.8
Fifty banks (entire test group)				
Total time (in hours)	2,635	2,937	−302	−10.3
Loans examined (in thousands of dollars)				
Commercial	52,223	60,607	−8,384	−13.8
Real estate	32,726	27,959	4,767	17.0
Consumer	3,555	4,993	−1,438	−28.8
Total	88,504	93,559	−5,055	−5.4
Loan coverage (in percent)				
Commercial	67	78	−11	
Real estate	77	66	11	
Consumer	13	18	−5	
Total	60	63	−3	

[a]For aggregate data on actual evaluations, see Appendix 2D.
[b]The difference as a percentage of actual evaluation figures.

Overall loan coverage declines from 63 percent to the 60 percent coverage requirement. This decline clearly contributes to the reduction in evaluation time. The other factor that contributes to the reduction in examination time is the shift from commercial and consumer loans to real estate loans. This shift occurs because the selection criterion in Version 1 is time minimization, and because the average evaluation time (minutes per $1000) for real estate loans for most banks in the test group was smaller than the evaluation time for commercial and consumer loans.[h]

The test results for Version 2 are presented in Table 2-5 for thirty-seven of the fifty banks. Thirteen banks are omitted from the second run because the coverage requirements could not be met

[h]As shown in Appendix 2D, the average evaluation time is 1.8, 1.2, and 6.7 minutes per $1000 of commercial, real estate, and consumer loans, respectively.

within the actual time spent in reviewing the loan portfolios.[1] These are the cases that, in Version 1, indicated a need for an increase in loan evaluation time.

Solving the second version of the model for thirty-seven banks results in an average improvement of 15.7 percent in the quality of coverage as measured by the expected value of classified loans. Only two cases show a decrease in the quality of coverage, while improvements ranging from about 1 percent to over 100 percent are indicated for thirty-five banks. This improvement is achieved by a shift from real estate loans, which have the lowest classification ratio, to commercial and consumer loans. The overall coverage is 69 percent, only 1 percent less than the actual coverage.

The overall results of the tests show that, even with the most simple versions of the model and with uniform coverage requirements, a time saving or an improvement in coverage can be obtained. The conflicting changes in coverage (from real estate loans to the other categories and vice versa) between Versions 1 and 2 of the model indicate that both time and quality of coverage have to be considered simultaneously. Moreover, the wide variations in the results suggest that substantial improvements can be obtained by tailoring the model for individual banks.

Implementation

The first implementation step involves the selection of a specific model. The choice of which version to use should be based on the objectives of the evaluation and on the policies of the organization performing the loan review. It is important that the selected model be as simple as possible. Models other than Versions 1 and 2 could be developed to replace or supplement these basic versions, provided they are both applicable and efficient.

One possible approach to the selection of a specific model is to start with a single or combined version, based on those presented in this chapter. When the user gains enough experience, he can modify this initial version in order to improve its efficiency.

---

[1] An infeasible solution of this type does not mean, of course, that the model cannot be solved. It simply indicates that the time constraint and/or the coverage constraints should be relaxed. Such changes were not introduced for the thirteen banks in order to maintain the same coverage and time requirements for all fifty banks.

Table 2-5
Model Results Compared to Actual Evaluations: Version 2—Thirty-Seven Banks

			Difference	
	Model	Actual evaluation	Amount	Percentage[a]
Total classified loans (in thousands of dollars)	3,434	2,968	466	15.7
Loans examined (in thousands of dollars)				
Commercial	50,253	45,591	4,662	10.2
Real estate	16,973	22,826	−5,853	−25.6
Consumer	4,335	3,840	495	12.9
Total	71,561	72,257	−696	−1.0
Loan coverage (in percent)				
Commercial	88	80	8	
Real estate	56	76	−20	
Consumer	27	24	3	
Total	69	70	−1	

[a]The difference as a percentage of actual evaluation figures.

Once a specific model, or set of models, has been derived, it becomes necessary to obtain the appropriate input data. These data can be divided into two major groups: the first group includes inputs based on actual loan evaluation data, and the second group includes subjective inputs determined by bank loan review officers or bank examiners.

The first group of data includes parameters that change from one loan review to another, as well as those that are more stable. The inputs that tend to change include, primarily, the volume of loans in each category. This information can be easily obtained from bank ledgers. Inputs that do not change frequently are the time required to evaluate each type of loan (T_i) and the ratio of classification (P_i). Information on time requirements can be obtained from the past data of each bank, from a cross-section analysis using a least-squares regression, from time studies, or from subjective estimates. Which of these methods is used will depend on the availability of data and on the type of model that is selected for implementation. There is no need for absolute accuracy in these figures as long as they are determined in the same way for all types of loans. The same theory applies to classification ratios (P_i), which can be best estimated by a time-series analysis of each bank.

The second type of data includes subjective parameters, such as coverage requirements that are likely to appear in any loan selection model. These parameters should be determined by bank management or by bank examiners. For practical purposes, it is suggested that low coverage levels be set for each loan category and that a higher coverage limit be set for total loans (as in the tests). In this way, the loans that have to be evaluated above the individual minimal bounds are optimally allocated among all the loan categories.

The loan selection model can be solved on any computer with an adequate linear programming subroutine. Hence, the solution itself does not present any problem. The model can be solved either at the main office or at a branch (if it is equipped with a computer terminal). The advantage of the first alternative is the availability of centralized data; local solutions have the advantage of faster, on-line modifications at the time of the actual loan review.

The solution indicates the dollar amount and/or the number of loans to be evaluated in each category, but the actual selection of specific loans is made by the user. The actual selection procedure varies according to the breakdown of the loan portfolio. Therefore, suggestions for this aspect of the implementation can be provided only for Versions 1 and 2, although other selection procedures are unlikely to be substantially different.

The proposed selection procedure requires that the model be solved in terms of both dollar amounts and number of loans; hence, the solution specifies the optimal amount and number of loans to be evaluated in the commercial, real estate, and consumer loan categories. The selection of specific loans in each of these three categories should follow a number of steps:

1. Evaluate all past due loans, previously scheduled loans, and all other special cases.
2. Subtract the amount and number of loans reviewed in step 1 from the optimal solution. The differences represent the amount and the number of loans that have to be selected.
3. In the commercial loans category, select the largest loans until the dollar value requirement is satisfied. Then take a random

sample from all the remaining loans in order to cover the required number of loans. (In this category, a number of loans extended to a single borrower is considered as one loan.)

4. In the two remaining categories, select a random sample of loans until the dollar requirement is satisfied.

This approach assures an adequate assessment of the short-run quality of the loan portfolio by evaluating the largest commercial loans. It also provides information about the long-run prospects of the bank by an evaluation of a random sample of all types of loans. The statistical significance of this sample can be established quite easily. Given the size of the population, the sample size, and the number of classified loans, it is possible to determine the confidence limits of the classification rate for the entire population of loans belonging to the same category. Obviously, if the population of a certain category is relatively small and if, because of time limitations or other constraints, the sample size is low, the range between the confidence limits may be quite wide. Nevertheless, the projection of the sample results on the relevant population provides information that is currently unavailable and that enables the user to increase a certain sample if the results are unacceptable.

Appendix 2A:
Notation

Time and Distribution Survey of Commercial Bank Loans Examination

Bank _____

Examiner in Charge _____

Date _____

Examination			This Examination			Last Examination		
Item	Type of loan		Commercial	Real estate	Consumer	Commercial	Real estate	Consumer
1	Total loans	Number (No.)	n_1	n_2	n_3			
		Dollars ($)	L_1	L_2	L_3			
2	Cutoff level	$						
3	Loans examined in detail	No.	e_1	e_2	e_3			
		$	E_1	E_2	E_3	A_1	A_2	A_3
4	Total classified loans	No.	c_1	c_2	c_3	s_1	s_2	s_3
		$	C_1	C_2	C_3	S_1	S_2	S_3
5	New classified loans (Not classified last time)	No.						
		$						
6	Loans examination time —Examiners	hours	h_1	h_2	h_3			
7	Loans examination time —Assistant examiners	hours						

Additional Notation [a]

$T_i = 60h_i/E_i$, $\quad L = L_1 + L_2 + L_3$, $\quad t_i = 60h_i/e_i$, $\quad n = n_1 + n_2 + n_3$, $\quad P_i = C_i/E_i$, $\quad E = E_1 + E_2 + E_3$, $\quad Q_i = S_i/A_i$, $\quad e = e_1 + e_2 + e_3$.

Survey form prepared by _____.

Time spent on survey preparation: _____ hours.

[a] h_i represents the sum of examiners' and assistant examiners' loan examination time (Items 6 and 7) for category i.

Appendix 2B:
Data for Numerical Example

Time and Distribution Survey of Commercial Bank Loans Examination

Bank _____

Examiner in Charge _____   Date _____

Examination		This Examination			Last Examination		
Item	Type of loan	Commercial	Real estate	Consumer	Commercial	Real estate	Consumer
1	Total loans — Number (No.)	583	96	931	Unknown	Unknown	Unknown
	Dollars ($)	4,365,113	679,770	778,384	3,515,377	412,387	644,735
2	Cutoff level $	7,500	7,500	7,500	5,000	5,000	5,000
3	Loans examined in detail — No.	210	54	30			
	$	3,764,626	626,861	59,314	3,247,184	327,492	56,793
4	Total classified loans — No.	8	1	0	3	0	9
	$	366,382	11,347	0	47,737	0	1,930
5	New classified loans (Not classified last time) — No.	7	1	0			
	$	336,431	11,347	0			
6	Loans examination time —Examiners hours	60	34	5			
7	Loans examination time —Assistant Examiners hours	5	1	1			

Survey form prepared by _____.

Time spent on survey preparation: _____ hours.

All inputs are underlined.

ON AT 12:23

USER NUMBER—_____
SYSTEM—BASIC
NEW OR OLD—OLD
OLD PROBLEM NAME—LINPRO***
WAIT.

READY.

1000 DATA 1, 0, 0, 0, 1, 0, 0, 0, 1, 1, 0, 0, 0, 1, 0, 0, 0, 1, 1, 1, 1
10001 DATA 4365, 680, 778, 2182.5, 136, 77.8, 3493.8
10002 DATA −1.04, −3.35, −6.1
RUN

LINPRO 12:26

TYPE "2" FOR OUTPUT OF TABLEAUS AND BASIS AT EACH ITERATION, "1" FOR THE
BASIS ONLY, OR "0" FOR JUST THE SOLUTION. WHICH? 0

WHAT ARE M AND N OF THE DATA MATRIX? 7, 3

HOW MANY "LESS THANS," "EQUALS," "GREATER THANS"? 3, 0, 4

YOUR VARIABLES 1 THROUGH 3
SURPLUS VARIABLES 4 THROUGH 7
SLACK VARIABLES 8 THROUGH 10
ARTIFICIAL VARIABLES 11 THROUGH 14

ANSWERS:

VARIABLE	VALUE
8	1085.
10	700.2
4	1097.5
1	3280.
2	136
3	77.8
9	544

OBJECTIVE FUNCTION VALUE −4341.38

DUAL VARIABLES:

COLUMN	VALUE
4	0
5	2.31
6	5.06
7	1.04
8	0
9	0
10	0

TIME: 15 SEC

**Appendix 2D:
Data for Testing the
Model—Fifty Banks**

Time and Distribution Survey of Commercial Bank Loans Examination

Bank _____

Examiner in Charge _____

Date _____

Examination			This Examination			Last Examination[a]		
Item	Type of loan		Commercial	Real estate	Consumer	Commercial	Real estate	Consumer
1	Total loans	Number (No.)	21,785	6,841	26,898			
		Dollars ($)	77,839	42,183	27,488			
2	Cutoff level	$						
3	Loans examined in detail	No.	7,099	2,858	2,259			
		$	60,607	27,959	4,993			
4	Total classified loans	No.	391	63	316			
		$	3,145	302	373			
5	New classified loans (Not classified last time)	No.	165	19	90			
		$	1,650	129	160			
6	Loans examination time —Examiners	hours	1,549	351	334			
7	Loans examination time —Assistant Examiners	hours	283	192	228			

Average evaluation time (minutes per $1000): $T_1 = 1.8$, $T_2 = 1.2$, $T_3 = 6.7$.

Classification ratio (C_i/E_i in percent): $P_1 = 5.2$ $P_2 = 1.1$, $P_3 = 7.5$.

Survey form prepared by _____.

Time spent on survey preparation: _____ hours.

[a]Not available for all fifty banks.

3 Numerical Credit-Scoring Methods

Traditional procedures for evaluating a customer's credit worthiness are based on the skill and experience of a loan officer. His analysis follows a number of steps and is guided by some famous rules about the three, four, five, or more Cs of credit: character, capital, collateral, capacity, conditions, and so forth (see, for example, Ettinger and Golieb [26, pp. 12-16] and Zimmerman [63, p. 15]). In the first rule, psychological considerations are emphasized; in the second, economic analysis is performed; in the third, legal aspects are considered; and so on. While all of these tests, as well as other common procedures, are very important, they do suffer from certain limitations. First, the evaluation process is subjective rather than objective; second, analysis of information is made sequentially rather than simultaneously; third, the traditional evaluation process is costly and time consuming. Moreover, the traditional evaluation process is often removed from collection procedures, control systems, and overall credit policy.

Although human judgment should be exercised in evaluating credit worthiness, especially in the commercial field, the evaluation process can benefit from more quantification and the use of mathematical models. These models could serve as supplements, and not necessarily as substitutes, to the analysis performed by a loan officer. Numerical credit-scoring methods are an important analytical tool of this sort.

Several objectives can be achieved through the proper use of a credit-scoring model:

1. Improvement in the quality of credit evaluation.[a]
2. Reduction in evaluation time and costs.
3. Better utilization of loan officers' time and experience.

---

[a]Improvement in evaluation quality is evidenced by an increase in net income from loans. In practice, a net increase in income can be achieved either through a reduction of bad debts accompanied by a reduction in credit volume, or through an increase in volume with a minimal increase in bad debts. Only in a few cases will a credit-scoring model enable a simultaneous reduction in charge-offs and an increase in volume.

4. Improvement in control over the credit portfolio, in general, and on individual branches and loan officers, in particular.
5. Facilitation of changes in credit policy.
6. Identification of potentially good customers to whom more credit can be sold.
7. Formalization of the credit evaluation procedure.

While this list of objectives may seem ambitious, an increasing number of commercial banks, finance companies, department stores, and other organizations have found that numerical credit-scoring models can fulfill these objectives. According to Fair [28], at least one organization has been scoring credit applications for more than a decade; about four million applications were scored in 1969; and several organizations have realized savings of millions of dollars per year.

The purpose of this chapter is to present the concepts, principles, and procedures of developing and implementing a credit-scoring model. The chapter is intended primarily for those who are not familiar with the credit-scoring method, but it also mentions some new methodological developments, such as a more efficient method for estimating the probability of misclassifications, and some novel uses, such as evaluating loans to black businessmen and estimating recoveries from delinquent borrowers. The presentation is descriptive rather than mathematical. It emphasizes the use of numerical credit scoring in screening loan applications, which represents the most common use of this method. The application of credit scoring to the evaluation of existing loans is explored in Chapters 4 and 5.

Concepts and Principles

Given our limited understanding of the ways in which a borrower's ability to repay a loan may be affected by later changes in his situation, it is impossible to isolate perfectly those loans that will eventually run into difficulty from those that will not. Instead, we attempt to create procedures that will weed out as many bad risks as possible while including the maximum number of good accounts. These procedures are empirical in nature; that is, they are based on actual experience and not on a theory, since there are no laws of social science that can predict with certainty whether a newly made loan will eventually be paid off or not.

The purpose of a numerical credit-scoring model is, therefore, to identify and weigh those characteristics that best discriminate between acceptable and poor credit risks. At this point, an acceptable credit risk, or a "good" loan, is defined as a paid-up account, while a poor credit risk, or a "bad" loan, is defined as a charged-off case. These definitions will be refined later.

The general procedure followed in developing a credit-scoring model can be summarized in four major steps, some of which are performed simultaneously:

1. Identify the key elements that best differentiate between good and bad loans.
2. Assign a proper weight to each of the characteristics defined in step 1.
3. Obtain a score for every loan by multiplying each selected element by its weight and then adding the products. This score is a measure of payment potential.
4. Compare the score to two predetermined cutoff levels and classify the loan accordingly into one of three categories: accepted (score above higher cutoff), rejected (score below lower cutoff), or subjected to further analysis (score between cutoff levels).

In essence, this procedure performs scientifically what a loan officer performs subjectively. It has the advantages of being more accurate, using various statistical techniques, and considering simultaneously all the borrower's characteristics—a task that is beyond the capabilities of the best loan officer. Let us discuss briefly each of the four phases in the credit-scoring process.

A typical consumer loan application contains dozens of items that can be divided into four major groups:

1. Personal data: age, sex, marital status, dependents, and so on.
2. Residential data: buy or rent, time at present address, type of neighborhood, and so on.
3. Occupation: income, time at present job, type of occupation, and so on.
4. Credit record: bank account, credit references, and so on.

As far as the credit-scoring model is concerned, these characteristics are important only if they help differentiate between good and bad credit risks. Table 3-1 presents the average values of several characteristics for a group of bad loans and a group of good loans. From the table, it can be seen that, in this particular case, the difference between the two groups is quite large in some elements, such as home ownership or bank references, and small in others, for example, marital status and possession of a telephone. To obtain an efficient credit-scoring model, only the best discriminating characteristics are selected and combined into one formula.[b] Normally, fewer than twenty elements are sufficiently discriminating, and most models incorporate not more than ten elements. This is also explained by the fact that certain characteristics are strongly dependent on each other; therefore, not more than one of each group of interdependent elements is included in the model.

Once the key elements have been defined, it is necessary to assign a weight to each. The weights depend on the discriminating power of each characteristic, on the interdependencies among the selected characteristics, and on the size and sign of each element. Thus, an element that is large for bad loans and small for good accounts will get a negative weight and vice versa. Technically, the selection and the weighting of the characteristics are done at the same time, with the use of multivariate statistical methods, such as discriminant analysis and regression analysis. These techniques consider all available elements and then take into account the combined effect that the selected characteristics have on credit quality. In this way, a credit-scoring model captures the multidimensional aspect of credit evaluation.

Given the selected variables and their appropriate weights, the score of an application can be computed in less than a second on a modern electronic computer and in a matter of minutes on a desk calculator. The entire range of characteristics is thus translated into a single score that represents the loan quality.

The final step involves a comparison between a loan's score and two cutoff levels. If the score exceeds the higher level, the loan application is automatically accepted, subject to verification of certain information such as employment and address. If the score falls below the lower cutoff level, the application is immediately rejected. If the score falls between the two cutoff levels, the application is

---

[b]It should be noted that the best discriminating characteristics may vary from one geographical area to another and even among different institutions in the same area. Hence, each financial institution should develop its own credit-scoring model.

Table 3-1
Profiles of Good and Bad Loans

Characteristic (variable)	Percentages of loans having these characteristics	
	Good Risks	Bad Risks
Is married	90.5	86.2
Owns his home	80.4	42.3
Owns his auto	80.7	68.0
Age is thirty-five or over	97.0	89.5
Has lived at least three years at present address	91.8	70.3
Has a bank reference	93.6	71.0
Has a telephone	75.4	70.3
Has fewer than three children	65.8	49.3

Source: William P. Boggess, "Screen-Test Your Credit Risks," *Harvard Business Review* (November-December 1967), p. 116.

transferred to an experienced loan officer for further analysis. Thus, loan officers can concentrate on marginal or unusual cases.

The main criterion used in defining the cutoff levels is the ratio between the profit from a good loan and the loss from a bad loan. The cutoff levels also depend on the expected proportion of bad loans, which is based primarily on the past experience of the lending organization. Other effects influencing this decision are the credit policy of the institution and the availability of credit. Cutoff levels may be lowered, for instance, for promotional purposes or raised because of tight monetary conditions.

Methodology

The Data

Since the numerical credit-scoring method is empirical in nature, the basis for developing such models is the available data on existing and past loan accounts. These historical data determine the range of variables that can be incorporated in a model and serve as a basis for determining both the cutoff levels and the weights of selected variables. Hence, the shape, depth, and availability of data play an important role in developing a credit-scoring model.

Using data on existing and historical accounts introduces a certain bias since only loans that passed the existing screening procedure are subject to selection and model development. Since the population of incoming applications is different from that of approved applications, the resulting credit-scoring model may be inadequate for screening purposes. This problem is minor if the proportion of rejections is relatively small, but it may become serious if the historical rejection rate was high. There are, however, several ways to reduce the biases caused by this problem (see Cohen and Hammer [16, p. 130]). One possible solution is to include all rejected applications in the group of bad accounts, assuming that all rejected accounts would have ended up as charge-offs. It is not likely that this will be the case, however, as evidenced by approved applications that end up as bad debts. An alternative solution requires that all applications be approved for a certain period and that the data for developing the model be obtained only from these loans. This approach is both time consuming and expensive since it may result in a substantial amount of bad debts.[c] It is preferable, therefore, to solve this problem in the implementation stage by considering the specific situation of individual institutions. At this point, it is assumed that all the data are obtained from loan accounts that have been approved under the existing evaluation system.

The first step in approaching the data is to define the two major populations involved, that is, good and bad accounts. Normally, a paid-up loan is defined as a good account and a charged-off loan (that is, a loan transferred to a collection department) is defined as bad. A better classification is based on account profitability; namely, a profitable account is defined as good, and an unprofitable account as bad. Thus, a loan submitted for collection but later repaid in full, including interest, penalty, and all additional expenses, may well be defined as good. Conversely, a loan account with constant delays that require numerous late-payment notices and a close follow-up may result in a net loss to the lender; thus, it may be defined as bad even if it is paid-up and never submitted for collection. In practice, however, most charged-off cases result in a net loss, and most paid-up cases in a net profit. Moreover, it is very difficult to measure the collection and follow-up costs per account. For these reasons, it is both easier and sufficiently accurate to define loan quality by the charge-off criterion.

---

[c]This was the experience of several commercial banks that have distributed large quantities of unsolicited credit cards and suffered substantial losses from these accounts.

Given the two loan populations, the necessary samples for developing and testing the model should be determined by standard statistical sampling methods. At this stage, two separate samples are defined. The first, *original*, sample is used to develop the credit-scoring model, while the second, *holdout*, sample is put aside for testing the complete model. This procedure is necessary to avoid biases that might occur if the model is tested with the same data that were used for its derivation.[d]

Two problems are likely to arise before the samples are determined and selected: first, the number of charged-off loans is quite small in most lending institutions; second, the populations of both good and bad loans may be heterogeneous rather than homogeneous. The first problem is important because it may result in a large difference between the number of good and bad loans in the samples. Such a disparity is likely to result in poor discrimination between the two groups.[e] Consequently, the entire population of bad loan accounts is normally selected. Then, a random sample of a similar size is selected from the paid-up accounts.[f]

The second sampling problem arises from heterogeneity in the loan portfolio. Although attributes such as size and repayment terms are normally quite homogeneous in consumer credit, there are variations in loan purposes and differences among loans that were made in different time periods. It is possible, for instance, that the repayment potential of loans made for health purposes is different from that of automobile loans. Thus, it is desirable to match good and bad accounts according to loan type by using the following procedure: first, all charged-off accounts are selected (or randomly sampled if the population of bad loans is large enough) and the number of cases belonging to each loan category is recorded; second, the population of good loans is stratified by loan types; finally, good accounts are randomly selected from each stratum so that the number of good and bad loans of each type is equal. To avoid biases resulting from changes in credit policy or economic conditions, it is also important

---

[d]The model can also be tested by an alternative method that does not require a holdout sample and that provides almost unbiased results. This method was developed by Lachenbruch [41] and will be presented later in the methodology section.

[e]Morrison [48, p. 160] points out that when one group is much larger than the other, almost all the observations are classified as the larger group.

[f]If historical data on paid-up loans are not available, good loans may be sampled from outstanding current accounts that are close to maturity and have, based on management evaluation, a high probability of being paid in full.

to make sure that both populations contain loans that were made approximately in the same period. While it is possible to stratify the loan portfolio into other categories, matching loans by type and time period is normally sufficient.

After solving the loan selection problem, it is necessary to decide what data should be obtained for each selected account. Three sources of data on loan accounts are normally available: the application form, external credit reports, and internal performance information. The last source is very useful for a scoring model designed for review or examination of existing loans but not for screening new loan applications. The second type of information is available from credit bureaus and from other financial institutions. When credit scoring is being used, however, this information is obtained only for marginal cases that require additional analysis. Thus, the major source of information that is relevant both for screening new loan applications and reviewing existing loan accounts is the application form. This source is the basis for defining the variables that are incorporated in the model.

The Variables

A credit-scoring model is based on a discriminating formula that has one dependent or explained variable and several independent or explaining variables. The dependent variable represents loan quality, that is, whether loans are good or bad.[g] The independent variables are used to estimate the dependent variable, that is, to predict loan quality. For instance, if borrowers' annual income has an important impact on the chances of collecting the loan, then annual income is incorporated in the model as one of the independent variables. The variables that are included in the model provide the best discrimination between good and bad loans. They are selected from a large variety of characteristics that are expected to affect loan quality.

A typical loan application includes many details from which

---

[g]Instead of using a dichotomous dependent variable that distinguishes only between two types of loans, it is possible to use a continuous variable to represent loan quality. Hattenhouse and Wentworth [32, p. 32], for example, suggest using the discounted rate of return on loans as the dependent variable. Because of the difficulties in obtaining the necessary information for calculating this type of variable, most credit-scoring models are based on a dichotomous decision variable.

dozens of independent variables can be defined. (Appendix 3A presents a list of items contained in an application form for consumer credit used by a medium-size commercial bank.) At an early stage of model development, it is desirable to define variables from most of the elements appearing on an application form so that potentially useful information will not be lost. At a later stage, irrelevant variables are discarded and only those contributing significantly to the discriminating formula remain in the model.

The definition of variables is straightforward for some items and more difficult for others. The first type of variables contains mostly quantitative elements, such as annual income, years with current employer, years at current address, and so on. The second type of variables contains qualitative items, such as home ownership, type of neighborhood, possession of a telephone, and bank accounts. The dependent variable (loan quality) is also included in this group. Most of these elements are phrased as yes or no questions for which dummy variables are defined.

Dummy variables may receive only two values, 1 or 0, which represent two possible answers to a question. For instance, home ownership may receive the value of 1, while renting is assigned the value of 0. Likewise, a "bad" neighborhood may be assigned the value of 0, as opposed to 1 for a "good" neighborhood. The same applies to loan quality, which may be assigned the value 1 for good loans and 0 for bad loans. It should be noted that the assignment of 0 to negative answers and 1 to positive ones is a matter of convenience only and could be reversed without any effect on the results, provided that it is done consistently for all the variables.

The main problem in defining dummy variables is to segregate all possible answers into two distinct categories. While this classification is simple for certain items, such as possession of a telephone, it is quite difficult for other elements, such as credit references and type of neighborhood. In the latter cases, it is necessary to classify in advance all possible answers into two categories, one for a positive effect, and the other for a negative effect on potential payoff. If this cannot be done, or if it causes the loss of important information, it is possible to define several dummy variables to represent more than two answers to a single question. This approach is relevant both for qualitative and quantitative items, as is explained below.

The use of dummy variables is not limited to qualitative variables. If it is assumed that certain quantitative variables do not vary continuously and linearly with the dependent variable (loan quality), they may be substituted by dummy variables. Consider the age variable, for example. If it is defined in terms of years, other things being equal, the payoff probability of an applicant who is fifty years old is twice as high as an applicant whose age is twenty-five and, likewise, an applicant who is seventy-five years old is a 50 percent better risk than a fifty-year-old borrower. This interpretation may be at odds with borrowers' repayment behavior, thus requiring a redefinition of the age variable by age groups rather than by years. It may be desirable, based on a rough knowledge of the borrowers' population and payment potential, to divide the age variable into five categories: up to twenty-five years, twenty-five to thirty-five, thirty-five to fifty, fifty to sixty-five, and over sixty-five years. As can be seen from this example, the range of years in each age group does not have to be equal. The next step is to define new variables to represent these five age categories.

In general, the division of one variable into n distinct categories requires the definition of $n-1$ dummy variables. Each of these variables receives the value of 1 if the observation falls within its range, and 0 if it belongs to one of the other $n-1$ classes. If the observation falls into the nth category, all $n-1$ variables receive the value of -1 (see Searle and Udell [58]). While other methods for performing this transition are available, the suggested approach avoids some of the biases introduced by other techniques. Using this method in the age characteristic example, four dummy variables replace the original continuous variable: if the applicant's age is thirty, for instance, the corresponding values of the dummy variables are 0, 1, 0, 0; for age fifty-three, the values are 0, 0, 0, 1; and for age sixty-six, -1, -1, -1, -1. A similar division into dummy variables can be applied to any quantitative and qualitative item that has a range of possible answers. In practice, however, dummy variables are used primarily for single-category qualitative elements corresponding to yes or no answers.

Multivariate Statistical Methods

When all the variables are defined, it is necessary to select and to weight the ones that best discriminate between good and bad loans. Both the selection and weighting are performed simultaneously with the use of multivariate statistical methods.[h] Two such methods are applicable to the development of credit-scoring models: discriminant analysis and regression analysis.

Discriminant analysis deals with three related statistical problems that apply to multivariate observations belonging to two or more groups. First, it distinguishes among groups and identifies group differences; second, it classifies existing and new observations into predetermined groups; finally, it identifies the key variables that contribute the most to the discrimination among groups (see Eisenbeis and Avery [24, p. 1]). Since the purpose of a credit-scoring model is to distinguish between good and bad loans where each observation contains many variables, it is obvious why discriminant analysis is applicable to this problem.

When only two categories are involved and the dependent variable is dichotomous (0 or 1), multivariate regression analysis provides identical results to those obtained from discriminant analysis (see Ladd [43]).[i] Since the credit-scoring problem has been defined in terms of two groups, both regression analysis and discriminant analysis can be used in developing a credit-scoring model. In fact, both techniques have been used extensively for this purpose. However, regression analysis has certain advantages over discriminant analysis: first, multivariate regression programs are more readily available for most computers; second, these programs are normally more sophisticated and contain more statistical information; and finally, they are better known to economists.[j]

One problem that has to be resolved prior to using either regression analysis or discriminant analysis is whether linear or quadratic functions should be used. Linear functions are obviously more simple to derive, but they can be used only if the two groups (good and bad loans) belong to two multivariate normal populations with

[h]An alternative, although less desirable, approach is first to select the discriminating variables using techniques such as factor analysis on principal component analysis and then to derive the weights of the selected variables. For an example of this approach, see Altman *et al.*[5].

[i]Another problem that arises from the use of dichotomous variables is that they are not normally distributed, as is assumed both in discriminant analysis and in regression analysis. However, Gilbert [29] demonstrated that functions with dichotomous variables can be used effectively in discriminant analysis.

[j]In recent years, the use of discriminant analysis in loan evaluation and related areas has increased substantially. This development can be attributed, primarily, to the use of discriminant analysis by Altman [3,4] in his studies of corporate bankruptcy and to the text by Eisenbeis and Avery [24] which contains a complete computer program for discriminant analysis.

equal dispersions (covariance matrices).[k] Since most of the existing credit-scoring models are based on linear classification rules, we concentrate our discussion on this procedure.[l]

If we assume that the dispersions of good and bad loans are equal, multivariate linear regression analysis can be used to derive the equation that provides the best differentiation between the two groups. This equation contains the independent variables that, as a group, provide the best discrimination between good and bad loans. The regression coefficients are the weights given to these variables and the computed value of the dependent variable represents the credit score.

The credit-scoring equation should be analyzed in the same way as the results from any regression program—namely, by checking the statistical significance of the coefficients (t test); by determining the contribution of each variable to the explanation of the dependent variable (contribution to R^2); by checking for intercorrelations among independent variables; by analyzing the sign of each coefficient; and so on. Since the main purpose of this regression is to predict, and since the resulting function is checked on a holdout sample, intercorrelations among independent variables may not be too serious a problem (see Johnston [39, p. 207]). The same applies to signs of explanatory variables, which may vary from expectations because of multicollinearity. It is preferable, however, to maintain the normal standards of regression analysis both for scientific and practical reasons.[m]

The Cutoff Levels

When multivariate regression analysis with a 0, 1 dependent variable is used, the resulting scores—that is, the computed values of the dependent variable—will concentrate between 0 and 1; but negative values and values larger than 1 are also possible. This range of values

[k]For a test of the equality of dispersion matrices, see Eisenbeis and Avery [24, p. 29].

[l]A notable exception is a study by Bates [9], who used quadratic classification rules in evaluating small loans to black and white businesses.

[m]In one organization where a credit-scoring model was developed, management was presented with four different scoring formulas. In examining these models, management considered not only differences in prediction quality but also the variables contained in each model. In particular, the model that provided the best prediction was rejected because it included certain items whose weights seemed bizarre to loan officers (see Myers and Forgy [50, p. 805]).

can be divided into two or three sections by using one or two cutoff levels. If the value of 0 is assigned to bad loans and 1 to good loans, and a single cutoff is used, then all applications with scores below the cutoff level are rejected, and applications with scores higher than the cutoff are accepted. More sophisticated credit-scoring models include a second cutoff level where all applications with scores below the lower level are rejected, those with scores higher than the upper level are accepted, and applications with scores lying between the two levels are subjected to further analysis.

The definition of cutoff levels is quite complex because the scores of good and bad loans usually overlap. This can best be seen from a frequency distribution of credit scores. Two sets of frequency distributions for good and bad loans are presented in Figures 3-1 and 3-2. The two sets differ in the degree of overlap between good and bad loans: in the first case (Figure 3-1), there is relatively little overlap, and in the second case (Figure 3-2), which is more common, the degree of overlap is substantial.

The usual objective in defining the cutoff level(s) is to minimize the probability of misclassification. When a single cutoff level is placed at the intersection of the two distributions (s_0 in Figure 3-1), the entire overlap area represents misclassifications. When two cutoff levels are defined, the loans belonging to the area between the cutoff levels (s_1 and s_2 in Figure 3-2) are subjected to additional analysis by loan officers or bank examiners. Immediate errors are represented by the misclassified areas to the left of the lower cutoff level and to the right of the upper cutoff level.

Misclassifications by credit-scoring models with one cutoff level are caused by two different types of errors: (1) bad loans classified as good and (2) good loans classified as bad. The first type of error results in charge-offs and collection costs and the second type of error results in lost revenues. Since these costs are not the same, it is insufficient to minimize the number of misclassified loans. Instead, the overall misclassification cost, which is equal to the number of errors of each type multiplied by their respective costs, has to be minimized. Hence, it is necessary to estimate the average loss from a bad loan and the average profit from a good loan.

In consumer credit, the loss from a charge-off account is, on the average, five times larger than the gain from a good account. There-fore, it may be desirable to raise the cutoff level in order to eliminate as many bad loans as possible at the expense of rejecting some good

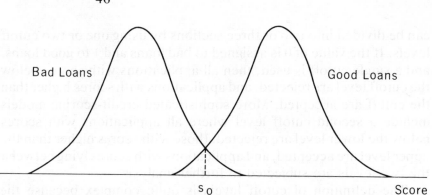

Figure 3-1. Frequency Distribution of Credit Scores for Good and Bad Loans—Small Overlap

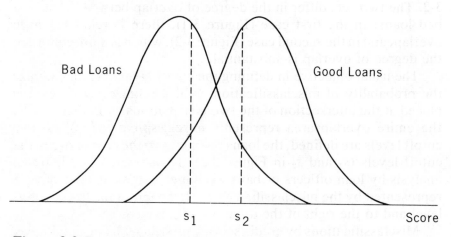

Figure 3-2. Frequency Distribution of Credit Scores for Good and Bad Loans—Large Overlap

loans. This process can best be illustrated by the cumulative distribution of credit scores (Figure 3-3): an increase in the cutoff level from s_1 to s_2 results in increasing the rejection rate of good loans from P_1 to P_2 and that of bad loans from Q_1 to Q_2.

It should be remembered that the cumulative distributions apply to each type of loan and not to the entire portfolio. Namely, the proportion of bad loans with scores lower than s_1 is Q_1 and the proportion of good loans with scores lower than s_1 is P_1. A random sample of loans from the entire portfolio is likely to contain a proportion of loans with scores lower than s_1 that is much closer to

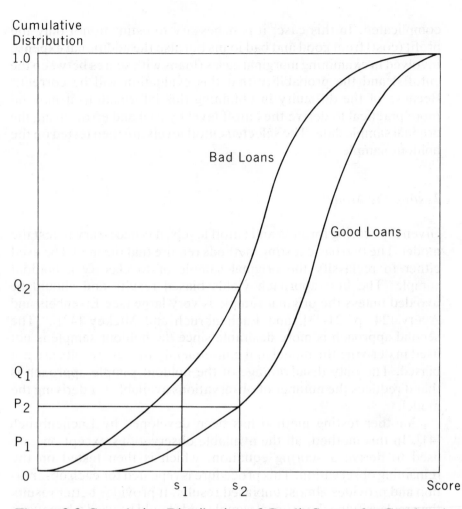

Figure 3-3. Cumulative Distribution of Credit Scores for Good and Bad Loans

P_1 than to Q_1, since the portion of bad accounts in an average portfolio is quite small. It is clear, therefore, that in order to derive the optimal cutoff level it is necessary to estimate not only the expected cost of a bad loan and the expected profit from a good loan but also the average proportion of bad accounts in the entire loan population.[n]

When two cutoff levels are used, their derivation is even more

[n]An optimal solution to this problem based on a continuous cost function is derived by Cohen and Hammer [16, pp. 131-134].

complicated. In this case, it is necessary to estimate not only the profit (cost) from good and bad loans but also the additional expense involved in examining marginal cases (loans with scores between the cutoffs) and the probability that this evaluation will be correct.[o] Because of the difficulty in obtaining this information, it may be more practical to derive the cutoff level by trial and error, using the original sample data. The selected cutoff levels are then tested on the holdout sample.

Testing the Model

Given the scoring formula and cutoff levels, it is necessary to test the model. The two basic testing methods require that the model be used either to reclassify the original sample or to classify a holdout sample. The first approach yields biased results and should be avoided unless the original sample is very large (see Eisenbeis and Avery [24, p. 21-23], and Lachenbruch and Mickey [42]).[p] The second approach is more desirable since the holdout sample is not used in deriving the model and consequently the test results are not biased. The only disadvantage of the holdout sample approach is that it reduces the number of observations available for deriving the model.

Another testing method has been developed by Lachenbruch [41]. In this method, all the available observations except one are used to derive a scoring equation, which is then tested on the remaining observation. This procedure is repeated for each observation and provides almost unbiased results. It provides better results than reclassifying the original sample and should be used whenever a holdout sample is not available.[q]

If the test results are satisfactory—that is, if the classification errors are within acceptable limits—the model is ready for implementation. If the results are not satisfactory—for example, if a large number of good loans are rejected for every bad loan that is

---

[o]For a presentation containing this information, see the section on "Implementation" in Chapter 4.

[p]Even if the original sample is large, it is preferable to use only part of the observations for deriving the model and to maintain the remaining observations for testing the model.

[q]The equation that is actually incorporated in the scoring model is based on all the observations. For an application of this method to a credit evaluation problem, see Eisenbeis and Murphy [25].

rejected—the model must be checked for possible biases resulting from various reasons such as strong intercorrelations among independent variables. After corrections are made—for instance, by eliminating existing variables and adding new ones—the revised model has to be retested until the outcome is satisfactory.

Implementation

The first issue to be resolved in implementing a credit-scoring model is how to replace an existing evaluation system with a new one. One possible approach is to use as input for the credit-scoring model only applications that were approved by a loan officer. It is obvious, however, that this approach does not achieve the main goal of substituting a subjective evaluation system with a mathematical model, even if a two-phase evaluation procedure is more efficient than the current process. Instead, it is suggested that the credit-scoring model first be run in parallel to the existing process, where all new applications serve as input. All credit-granting decisions in which the model and loan officer agree would then be carried out. Disagreements would be resolved through further analysis, and, after a while, the information and experience gathered through this joint operation would be used to change the model, if necessary. Then the revised model would be used exclusively, and loan officers would devote all of their time to marginal cases.

The screening procedure with a credit-scoring model is very simple. Every new application is scored and classified into one of three groups: approvals, marginals, or rejects. The information on a rejected application is maintained, but no further action is taken. A marginal case is transferred to an experienced loan officer for further analysis, which normally requires additional information. An approved application is subjected to verification of certain key items, such as employment and residence. In addition, an approved application may be checked to find out if it contains adverse information on items not included in the model. For instance, if the income variable is not included in the model, it is necessary to examine whether income is sufficient to service monthly loan payments. In a sophisticated credit-scoring model, all of these checks are programmed and incorporated into the model.

An efficient credit-scoring model should be accompanied by an up-to-date information system. This system should contain a data bank and all relevant reports. The data bank should incorporate the original information from all applications and data on payments, late payment notices, collections, and so on. All information on rejects, charge-offs, and payoffs should be maintained for a predetermined period. This data bank provides the basis for reviewing, updating, and testing the model periodically.

The reporting system serves as an important control device for management. Reports may include the scores of all loans approved, rejected, or further analyzed in each branch and by each loan officer. The reports also contain information on charge-offs, rejections, and various summaries and statistical analyses that help top management to review and, if necessary, to alter the credit policy of the institution.

Uses and Applications

In addition to screening new consumer loan applications, credit-scoring models can be used as important aids in many tasks, mostly related to the loan function. Some of these are:

1. Determining the size of down payment.
2. Determining the amount of deposit for public utilities.
3. Determining the terms of credit cards—for example, the credit limit.
4. Determining the amount of information that should be purchased from credit bureaus.
5. Estimating potential recoveries from delinquent borrowers.
6. Screening trade credit applications.
7. Screening small business loan applications.
8. Scoring municipal and industrial bonds.
9. Reviewing outstanding commercial loans (see Chapter 4).
10. Reviewing outstanding consumer loans (see Chapter 5).[r]

While some of these uses have already been implemented, others are in the development stage. It is expected that additional uses will

---

[r]For a discussion of items 1-4, see Myers [49, p. 6]; for item 5, see Lane [44]; for 6, see Ewert [27]; for 7, see Edmister [21, 22] and Bates [9]; for 8, see Carleton and Lerner [14], Horton [33] and Pinches and Mingo [55].

be developed as credit-scoring models become more widespread.

One of the first reported applications of a credit-scoring model was performed in 1941 by Durand [20], for consumer installment loans, but even earlier reports on this subject are known (for example, see Dunham [19]). With the rapid development of electronic computers and the widespread use of management science models, numerical credit-scoring applications increased in the fifties and primarily in the sixties. They are now being used by commercial banks, finance companies, mail-order houses, department stores, gasoline companies, and other retail and financial organizations. Credit-scoring models are now being used not only by large institutions but also by small firms (see Appendix 3B—a scoring sheet of a small country bank).

Most users of credit scoring report on favorable results. Morris [47, p. 636] reports about a situation where 60-85 percent of all consumer loan applications were processed through a credit-scoring system, resulting in a 10-35 percent reduction of charge-offs with a minimal loss of business. Zaegal [62] reports that eighteen offices of American Investment Company of Illinois used a credit-scoring system for three years and had a 33 percent reduction in seriously delinquent accounts, while offices not using the system had a 4 percent reduction in the same period. Boggess [12, p. 121] comments on a case where the average evaluation time for new loan applications was reduced from one week to twenty-four hours under a new credit-scoring system. McGrath [46] reports that a scoring system for an automobile dealer reduced bad debts by 20 percent, with a 1 percent loss of potentially good accounts.

These favorable reports raise the questions of why it took so long to apply scoring systems and why they are not universally accepted. There are several reasons for this phenomenon (see Myers and Forgy [50, p. 800]): first, a reluctance to substitute subjective judgment with a mathematical formula; second, the lack of perfect scoring systems that can distinguish between good and bad loans with certainty; and, finally, the difficulties in "selling" the idea to management and actually implementing the model.

Concluding Comments

The empirical, rather than theoretical, approach followed in developing a credit-rating model has its disadvantages. Predictions are based on past experience and not on laws of social science. The results provide improvement over traditional procedures but no optimal solutions. Other limitations are, for example, using only approved applications as data, approaching individual loans rather than a whole portfolio, using dichotomous or polychotomous variables in multivariate regression analysis, and so on. While none of these problems should be overlooked, the potential payoff from an efficient credit-scoring system is large enough to warrant its development and installation.

Several important objectives can be reached through the efficient use of a credit-scoring model. First, the quality of credit evaluation can be improved, resulting in higher revenues and reduced processing costs. Second, the formalization of credit evaluation aids in training new loan officers and provides an important control device. Third, changes in credit policy can be translated into revised cutoff levels to obtain an immediate effect on the volume and composition of new loans. Fourth, the model identifies potentially good customers to whom more credit could be sold. Finally, the task of loan officers becomes more challenging, and the officers' experience is better utilized by enabling them to concentrate their efforts on marginal and special cases and to omit the large mass of routine applications.

The success of a credit-scoring model is not assured even if it has been carefully derived and tested. The implementation phase should be carefully planned and executed, with special emphasis on the behavioral aspects of changeover. Once a model has been installed, it should not be used mechanically. Instead, periodical review and reformulation, if necessary, should be part of the system to assure its long-run applicability and profitability.

Appendix 3A:
Typical Loan Application
Items

Personal

1. Full name.
2. Age.
3. Single, married, divorced.
4. Phone: home.
          business.
5. Dependents.
6. Home address.
7. Years there.
8. Purpose of loan.

Employment

1. Name of company
   or government department.
2. Years there.
3. Position.
4. Salary.
5. Other income.
6. Source.
7. Previous employer.
8. Years there.

Spouse

1. Age.
2. Where employed.

3. Years there.
4. Position.
5. Salary.
6. Previous employer.
7. Years there.

Bank References

1. Checking.
2. Savings.
3. Loans (list).

Real Estate

1. Location.
2. When purchased.
3. Cost.
4. First trust.
5. Second trust.
6. Monthly payments.

Present Automobile

1. Make.
2. Year.
3. Where financed.

Personal

1. Full name.
2. Age.
3. Single, married, divorced.
4. Phone home.
5. business.
6. Dependents.
7. Home address.
8. Years there.
9. Purpose of loan.

3. Years there.
4. Position.
5. Salary.
6. Previous employer.
7. Years there.

Bank Reference

1. Checking.
2. Savings.
3. Loans (if any).

Employment

1. Name of company or government department.
2. Years there.
3. Position.
4. Salary.
5. Other income.
6. Source.
7. Previous employer.
8. Years there.

Real Estate

1. Location.
2. When purchased.
3. Cost.
4. First trust.
5. Second trust.
6. Monthly payments.

Present Automobile

1. Make.
2. Year.
3. Where financed.

Spouse

1. Age.
2. Where employed.

Appendix 3B:
Credit-Scoring Worksheet Used by a Small Country Bank

Name _____ Date _____

					Score
Length of employment	10 years or more	5-10 years	3-5 years	1-3 years	
Score	100	75	50	25	_____
Length of residence	10 years or more	5-10 years	3-5 years	1-3 years	
Score	25	20	15	10	_____
Total annual income	Over $7500	$5000-$7500	$3600-$5000	$2400-$3600	
Score	100	80	60	40	_____
Age of purchaser	35 years or older	30-35 years	25-30 years	21-25 years	
Score	50	40	30	20	_____
Credit evaluation	Excellent	Good	Fair	Poor	
Score	125	90	60	25	_____
Sex and marital status	Male— married	Male— Other	Female— married	Female— other	
Score	25	0	25	25	_____
Phone	Has phone				
Score	50				_____
Bank account	Checking	Savings	Both	Bank name only	
Score	25	25	25	25	_____

Total score: _____

55

A Credit-Scoring Model for Commercial Loans

For several reasons, it is difficult to apply the credit-scoring method to the evaluation of commercial loans (see Hammer and Orgler [31]). First, the number of commercial borrowers is normally quite small compared to customers for consumer credit; thus, there is a problem in obtaining a sufficient number of observations for a statistically significant study. Second, there are substantial variations among commercial loans with respect to their size, terms, collateral, and payment procedures, all of which are relatively uniform in the case of consumer loans. Finally, there is a lack of reliable up-to-date financial data on commercial borrowers, particularly on small businesses and on firms that default on their loans.

Because of these problems, it is very difficult to develop a general credit-scoring model for commercial loan applications. This may be one of the reasons for the lack of analytical models in the commercial loan area. There are, however, several related studies that will be analyzed briefly. One important study of this type was performed by Altman [3]. Using discriminant analysis, Altman derived a discriminant function with only five variables, all of them financial ratios, and predicted corporate bankruptcy with a remarkable accuracy (14 percent error on a holdout sample of twenty-five bankrupt firms). This prediction was obtained with financial data one year prior to bankruptcy. However, longer lead times produced substantially higher error rates. Since commercial loans may result in a complete or partial loss several years before bankruptcy, or even without the borrower becoming bankrupt at all, Altman's model is not applicable to the credit scoring of commercial loans. A later study by Altman *et al.* [5] that was designed for evaluating commercial loan applications provided substantially inferior results compared with Altman's original study.

A model for screening trade credit applications by small firms, mostly one-owner retail stores, has been developed by Ewert [27].

This chapter is a revision of an earlier paper published in the November 1970 issue of the *Journal of Money, Credit and Banking*[52].

The applicants and the amounts involved more closely resemble consumer credit than average bank loans to commercial customers. Nevertheless, the model is useful for reviewing new customers for trade credit. The model combines information on the owner with data, from Dun and Bradstreet reports, on the financial position of the store. Other studies involving the derivation of credit-scoring models for small business loans were performed by Bates [9], Edmister [21, 22], and Abate [1]. Another interesting study was conducted by Cohen, Gilmore, and Singer [15], who developed a model that simulates the commercial lending decisions of bank loan officers. Consequently, the model is of a descriptive, rather than a normative, nature.

The purpose of this chapter is to present a general credit-scoring model for the evaluation of outstanding commercial loans. Although this objective is somewhat less ambitious than the derivation of a general model for screening new commercial loan applications, the model presented here provides a useful tool for loan review and examination. Because of the difference in objectives, this model is different from previous studies primarily in the selection of independent variables and also in the solution of particular problems that arise in developing a general model for a heterogeneous population of borrowers.

The Model

The model is developed according to the principles and procedures outlined in Chapter 3. Multivariate regression analysis is used to discriminate between good and bad loans. The independent variables represent various characteristics of the borrowers and their past loan performance, and the dichotomous dependent variable (Y_i) equals 1 for bad loans and 0 for good loans.[a] Since only two groups are involved, this technique provides the same results as discriminant analysis and it has the advantages of being more readily available, better known, and normally containing more statistical information.

The dichotomous dependent variable expresses the loan quality.

---

[a]It should be noted that the assignment of 1 to bad loans and 0 to good loans is a matter of convenience only. The values of this dummy variable can be reversed (as is done in the next chapter) without affecting the final results.

In this study, the definition of quality—that is, whether a loan is good or bad—was not based on actual payoff or charge-off. Instead, any loan criticized by a bank examiner was considered as bad and any loan evaluated but not criticized was classified as good. This operational definition was selected because of data availability and because a study by Wu [61] confirmed that examiners' criticism of business loans is a good predictive measure of loan quality. Moreover, even if a criticized loan is not charged-off, it is likely to cause additional expenses to the lender and to provide smaller earnings than good loans. Finally, both loan review officers and bank examiners are clearly interested in identifying this type of loan in a review or an examination.

Independent variables are divided into two major groups: the first contains financial ratios and other financial variables that are based on current and past financial statements of the borrowers. The second group contains loan performance variables as well as other variables that are expected to contribute to the prediction of loan quality. The information for calculating these variables is obtained from financial reports and examination reports—sources that are available both to loan review officers and bank examiners.

The first group contains numerous ratios that provide information on borrowers' liquidity, profitability, leverage, and activity. The main financial variables that were incorporated originally in the regression analysis are:

1. Liquidity: Current assets/current liabilities; working capital; cash/current liabilities; inventory/current assets; quick ratio; working capital/current assets.
2. Profitability: Net profit/sales; net profit/net worth; net profit/total assets; net profit $\geqq 0$; net profit.
3. Leverage: Net worth/total liabilities; net worth/fixed assets; net worth/long-term debt; net worth $\geqq 0$.
4. Activity: Sales/fixed assets; sales/net worth; sales/total assets; sales/inventory; sales/receivables.

These and other variables are derived from the last available financial statement prior to classification. Additional independent variables in this group are based on the differences between the last (t) and next-to-last ($t-1$) annual reports. Such differences may signal a deterioration or an improvement in the liquidity, profitability, or solvency of the borrower. Among these variables are current ratio

(t)/current ratio $(t-1)$; net profit $(t-1)$; [sales (t) − sales $(t-1)$]/sales $(t-1)$; total assets (t)/total assets $(t-1)$; and net worth (t)/net worth $(t-1)$.

The second group of variables contains information on the past performance of commercial loans and other elements that are considered useful in predicting loan quality. Most of these variables are based on the response to questions such as: Is the loan secured or unsecured? Has it been criticized by a bank examiner during the last examination? Has the loan balance fluctuated or has it increased steadily during last year? Is the firm incorporated? Are the latest financial statements available? Are they audited? Obviously, the answers to these questions are defined as dummy variables.[b]

After eliminating all the variables that do not contribute to the explanation of the variation in Y_i and that are not significantly related to Y_i, we obtain the credit-scoring function. The application of this equation to each observation provides a credit score. This score is used to decide whether a loan should be carefully evaluated or omitted from the review process.

The loan classification procedure is based on two cutoff levels, C_1 and C_2, where $C_1 < C_2$. Since in this study $Y_i = 1$ for bad loans and $Y_i = 0$ for good loans, any loan for which $\hat{Y}_i \geq C_2$ is potentially bad and requires a thorough evaluation, while observations for which $\hat{Y}_i \leq C_1$ are considered to be good and are eliminated from the review process. The remaining cases ($C_1 \leq \hat{Y}_i \leq C_2$) are marginal loans that are reviewed briefly and classified into one of the two other groups. Consequently, the loan review process has three stages: first, the model is used to classify the loans as good, marginal, or bad; second, a loan review officer or a bank examiner briefly reviews the marginal loans to determine whether they belong to the good or bad category; finally, the reviewer examines in detail all the loans in the bad category.[c] It is important to note that the classification of loans into three rather than only two categories (good and bad) is designed to

---

[b]While the independent variables are assumed to belong to multivariate normal populations, it has been shown by Gilbert [29] that functions with dichotomous variables can be used efficiently in discriminant analysis.

[c]A similar approach, although not based on credit scoring, has been suggested by Abdel-Khalik [2, p. 52] for screening commercial loan applications. According to his suggestion, commercial borrowers should first submit a condensed application form containing aggregated accounting information. Based on this form, a customer is classified as good, marginal, or bad. Good customers are approved, bad ones are rejected, and marginal borrowers are required to provide detailed accounting information for a detailed analysis. Abdel-Khalik admits that his recommendations are tentative since his study is based on four firms only.

increase the efficiency of the model. By providing an intermediate category to which all the marginal cases are classified and which is subject to a brief review, the number of immediate misclassifications is reduced substantially.

Because of the difficulties in deriving analytically the optimal values of the cutoff levels (see the subsection on "Cutoff Levels" in Chapter 3), the values of C_1 and C_2 in this study are based on an arbitrary decision rule. This rule specifies that the proportion of bad loans classified wrongly as good should be less than 5 percent of all bad loans and that the proportion of bad loans classified correctly as bad should be at least 75 percent of total bad loans (the remainder falls into the "marginal" category). The emphasis on bad loans is explained by the relatively high penalty cost associated with over-looking a potentially bad loan. In practice, some rough cost esti-mates should be used in determing the appropriate decision rule.

Using a trial-and-error approach, C_1 and C_2 are varied until the reclassified observations from the original sample satisfy the re-quirements of the decision rule.[d] The credit-scoring model, which contains the discriminating function and the cutoff levels, is then tested on the holdout sample. If the classification results of the holdout sample satisfy the constraints of the decision rule, the model is ready for implementation.

The Data

The data were obtained from the files of FDIC examiners in a number of East Coast states. Two major problems in obtaining the data were the lack of complete financial statements and the small number of criticized or bad loans. To obtain a sufficient number of observations, thousands of loan reviews in 100 state nonmember commercial banks were screened. Each observation had all the items mentioned in the previous section, including data from the next-to-last financial statements. While earlier reports were gener-ally not available, it turned out that they were unnecessary since none of the financial ratios with previous year $(t-1)$ variables were significant.

---

[d]Since the decision rule applies only to bad loans, the determination of C_1 and C_2 is based only on the reclassification of loans that were actually bad. Good loans are classified automatically according to the same cutoff levels.

62

Any bad loan for which all the necessary data were available was incorporated into the study. The control group of good loans was randomly selected from a stratified population of all the good loans with adequate data that were listed in the observed files of FDIC examiners. Good loans were stratified by industry because of the large variety of borrowers, and, for each bad loan in a certain industry, several good loans were randomly selected from the appropriate stratum. Loans were not matched by the size of the borrowing firms (neither by assets, sales, nor by other measures) since we were interested in the effect of size on the quality of commercial loans. Many types of industries were included, and total assets of individual firms ranged from $7500 to $11,623,900. This diversification served the purpose of developing a general credit-scoring model for existing loans.

The selected observations were randomly divided into two groups: an original sample and a holdout sample. The first group contains seventy-five bad loans and 225 good loans; that is, each bad loan was matched with three good loans in the same industry. This group provided the data for the regression analysis and for the definition of the cutoff levels. The effectiveness of the model was tested on the second group which contains forty bad loans and eighty matched good loans.

Empirical Results

The Credit-Scoring Function

The regression equation that provides the best discrimination between good and bad loans includes only six independent variables, which are listed in Table 4-1. Most of the independent variables that were originally incorporated into the model had insignificant coefficients and did not contribute to the explanation of the variation in the dependent variable (no contribution to R^2). Another group of variables was eliminated because of multicollinearity. While multicollinearity is acceptable when the main purpose of the regression is to predict, all the variables that have been eliminated improved only the prediction of the original sample and provided inferior results when tested on the holdout sample. Moreover, the coefficients of

Table 4-1
Regression Results: The Credit-Scoring Function

Variable	Coefficient	t Value
1. Secured/unsecured	0.1017	1.83[a]
2. Past due	−0.3966	−4.14
3. Audit	−0.0916	−2.01
4. Net profit ≤ 0	−0.1573	−2.96
5. Working capital/current assets	−0.0199	−3.28
6. Criticized last examination	−0.4533	−9.22
Intercept $= 1.1018$		
$R^2 = 0.364$		
$n = 300$.		

[a]Significant at the 10 percent level; all other variables are significant at 5 percent or better.

the variables rejected for multicollinearity had signs that could not be rationalized on a priori grounds.[e]

The signs of the regression coefficients (Table 4-1) are consistent with our expectations about the effect of each variable on loan quality:

1. $X_1 = 0$ for unsecured loans and $X_1 = 1$ for secured loans. Since the dependent variable is 0 for good loans and 1 for bad loans, a positive coefficient means that secured loans are more risky than unsecured loans. This result is somewhat surprising at a first glance; however, the need for a security is an indication that such a loan was considered more risky when it was originally made.[f]

2. $X_2 = 0$ for past-due loans and $X_2 = 1$ for current loans. It is obvious that when an interest payment is overdue, the likelihood of a loss is larger—hence the negative coefficient.

3. $X_3 = 0$ for a firm *not* audited and $X_3 = 1$ for an audited firm. It is expected that examiners have more confidence in the reliability of audited statments than in a borrower's unaudited statements. A negative coefficient confirms this expectation.

4. $X_4 = 0$ for a net loss and $X_4 = 1$ for a net profit. A negative coefficient for this variable is obvious. It is interesting that this variable provides better explanatory and predictive results than any of the other profitability ratios, whether independently or within the regression equation.

[e]A few additional regression equations that differed from the selected function in one or two variables provided similar but slightly inferior results.

[f]Senior bank officers and bank examiners expressed a similar view in a recent panel discussion on commercial lending [40, p. 38].

5. X_5 is the only independent variable that is not restricted to the values 0 and 1. Obviously, as the ratio of working capital (current assets less current liabilities) to current assets increases, the quality of the loan should increase and hence the negative coefficient. Slightly inferior results were obtained when X_5 was replaced with a dummy variable that, like X_4, applied only to the sign of working capital, that is, whether it is negative or positive. The use of dummy variables has, of course, the advantage of simplicity, and the variable is less sensitive to inaccuracies in the financial reports.

6. $X_6 = 0$ for loans criticized by a bank examiner during the last examination and $X_6 = 1$ for uncriticized loans. A previously classified loan is obviously of poor quality and hence the negative sign.[g]

Loan Classifications

By applying the decision rule specified in the section on "The Model" earlier in this chapter to the original sample data, we obtain the two cutoff levels:[h] $C_1 = 0.08$ and $C_2 = 0.25$. Classification results for the original sample based on these cutoff levels are presented in Table 4-2.

The results indicate that three of the actually bad loans are classified as good, twelve as marginal, and sixty as bad. The implication for review and examination purposes is that three bad loans will not be evaluated at all, and twelve such loans will be examined briefly, assuming that such an evaluation will suffice to identify them as potentially bad loans and to transfer them to the group of sixty loans designated for thorough analysis. Likewise, fifty-six good loans are eliminated from the review process, 123 are subjected to a brief analysis, and forty-six are classified as bad and require a

---

[g]Like the past-due status, a previous classification normally stimulates an evaluation during the next examination. It is important to note, however, that the regression equation provides a much better discrimination between bad and good loans than a simple rule that states that all past-due and previously classified loans are bad.

[h]Because of the small number of variables, of which only one is continuous, part of the classification can be done by a simple set of decision rules. For instance, all unsecured ($X_1 = 0$) current ($X_2 = 1$) loans that have not been previously criticized ($X_6 = 1$) and that were made to profitable borrowers ($X_4 = 1$) with audited financial statements ($X_3 = 1$) are classified as good. The same loan ($X_1 = 0$, $X_2 = 1$, $X_4 = 1$, and $X_6 = 1$) to a borrower with unaudited statements ($X_3 = 0$) and a working-capital to current-assets ratio of at least 0.75 ($X_5 \geq 0.75$) is the only other type of loan to be classified as good. Similar rules for marginal classifications are much more complex and are therefore impractical.

Table 4-2
Classification Results—Original Sample

	Prediction (in number of loans)				Prediction (in percentages)			
Actual	Bad	Marginal	Good	Total	Bad	Marginal	Good	Total
Bad	60	12	3	75	80.0	16.0	4.0	100.0
Good	46	123	56	225	20.4	54.7	24.9	100.0
Total	106	135	59	300	35.3	45.0	19.7	100.0

detailed evaluation. A better presentation of these results is provided in terms of percentage points (second part of Table 4-2).[i]

It is important to note that the proportional time saving from using the model, compared with a complete evaluation, is greater than is indicated by the bottom line of Table 4-2. The ratio of good to bad loans in the original sample is 3:1, while in an average loan portfolio this ratio is much higher. Thus, the percentage of loans completely eliminated from evaluation is closer to 24.9 percent rather than 19.7 percent, and the proportion of loans briefly analyzed is approximately 54.7 percent rather than 45.0 percent.

As explained in Chapter 3, the reclassification of the original sample is biased since the regression equation and the cutoff levels are based on the same data. A more rigorous test is performed by using the model to classify the observations in the holdout sample. The results, presented in Table 4-3, are somewhat better than the reclassifications of the original sample. Good loans are classified more accurately in each of the three categories, and the percentage of bad loans classified as good is reduced from 4.0 to 2.5 percent. Only the classification of bad loans as bad is somewhat smaller because of an increase in the marginal classifications. Since the results satisfy the requirements of the decision rule, the model is considered applicable to the same type of institutions from which the data were obtained.[j]

[i]It should be noted that the classification results for bad loans are slightly better than the requirements specified by the decision rule. This outcome is caused by discontinuities in the credit scores that enable an improvement in the classification of one category without adverse effects on the other category. In this case, it was possible to achieve a small improvement in the classification of bad loans without adversely affecting the classification of good loans.

[j]This conclusion depends, of course, on our arbitrary decision rule. If this rule is inadequate for certain institutions it has to be changed, resulting in different cutoff levels that have to be tested in the same fashion. It is unlikely, however, that such a change will have an adverse effect on the general applicability of the model.

Table 4-3
Classification Results—Holdout Sample (in percentages)

| | Prediction | | | |
Actual	Bad	Marginal	Good	Total
Bad	75.0	22.5	2.5	100.0
Good	17.5	47.5	35.0	100.0
Total	36.7	39.2	24.1	100.0

Implementation

An implementation of the model depends on data availability and cost considerations. The necessary data for calculating the six variables in the scoring function are readily available. Moreover, the model is very simple and the credit score ($\hat{Y}_i$) can be easily computed on an adding machine. In a large bank, the computation can be performed by a computer, and, if the loan portfolio is maintained on auxiliary storage, the credit score can be computed periodically. The output of such a program will include a listing of potentially bad and marginal loans. In addition, the output may include the necessary information for analyzing the marginal cases.

The only major problem in implementing the model is the definition of C_1 and C_2. Theoretically, the optimal cutoff levels can be derived analytically by minimizing total evaluation costs (see Cohen and Hammer [16, pp. 131-134]). However, this procedure is based on the functional relationship between the evaluation cost and the credit scores. Unfortunately, the empirical derivation of this function is extremely difficult.

An alternative approach is to use the original sample and vary C_1 and C_2 until the average loan evaluation cost is minimized. The resulting values of C_1 and C_2 are then tested on the holdout sample and, if the results are satisfactory, they become part of the model. This trial-and-error procedure requires the following information:

1. The cost of eliminating a bad loan from consideration (F). This cost depends on the probability that the loan will actually be classified as bad if it is evaluated and on the savings that will result from such a classification.
2. The average evaluation cost per loan (E).

3. The proportion of time necessary to analyze a marginal loan relative to a detailed evaluation (p).
4. The a priori probability that a commercial loan will be criticized by a bank examiner (h).
5. The probability that a marginal loan will be transferred for a detailed evaluation (q_1 for loans that are actually bad and q_2 for good loans).

Given this information, the average evaluation cost per loan is:

$$K = \{E(Y_{bb} + pY_{bm} + q_1Y_{bm}) + F[Y_{bg} + (1 - q_1)Y_{bm}]\}h/Y_b$$
$$+ E(Y_{gb} + pY_{gm} + q_2Y_{gm})(1 - h)/Y_g,$$

where Y_{bb}, Y_{bm}, and Y_{bg} are the number of actually bad loans that are classified as bad, marginal, and good, respectively; and $Y_b = Y_{bb} + Y_{bm} + Y_{bg}$. Similarly, Y_{gb}, Y_{gm}, and Y_{gg} are good loans that are classified as bad, marginal, and good, respectively; and $Y_g = Y_{gb} + Y_{gm} + Y_{gg}$. The values of $Y_{bb}, \ldots, Y_{gg}$ are changed, by varying C_1 and C_2, until K is minimized.

If the above information is available, the cost of operating the model can be compared with the current cost of loan review or examination to determine whether the model is economically justifiable. For instance, if the current review process requires a detailed evaluation of every commercial loan and if the commercial loan portfolio contains N loans, the expected saving from using the model is $(E - K)N$. This saving is then compared with the cost of operating the model to determine whether the model contributes to a more efficient review process.

Unfortunately, it is not only difficult to estimate the functional relationship between K and Y_i, for an analytical derivation of C_1 and C_2, but it is also difficult to obtain all the necessary information for the alternative cost minimization approach. Consequently, it is necessary to define C_1 and C_2 by using a simple decision rule similar to the one used in this study.

Concluding Comments

Because of its simplicity and generality, the model presented in this chapter is applicable to most banks. The lack of standard review systems in many banks and the time pressure on examiners of bank regulatory agencies are two important reasons why such a model is necessary. The model can be applied to an entire commercial loan portfolio or to a random sample of loans that is selected, for example, by using the linear programming model presented in Chapter 2. In the latter case, the efficiency of the selection procedure is further improved by the model.

It is important to note that the model is not a substitute for a thorough loan evaluation. Its main purpose is to identify the most risky and potentially bad loans. The detailed evaluation is still performed by loan review officers and bank examiners. However, since the reviewers are relieved by the model from routine evaluations, they can allocate all their time to a small proportion of loans, that is, those that are most risky.

In addition to its normative value, the model provides some evidence on the relationship between loan classifications by bank examiners and information on the borrower. This result agrees with the expectations of Benston [10], who tried unsuccessfully to predict substandard loan classifications by factors related to individual banks. His main conclusion, which is confirmed by this study, is that the factors that influence substandard loans are related to the characteristics of the borrowers and not to those of the bank.

Credit-Scoring Models for Outstanding Consumer Loans

Outstanding consumer loans normally receive little attention from loan review officers and bank examiners because of the small size of these loans and the fact that potential difficulties are soon identified through missing payments. In recent years, however, the volume of consumer loans has increased substantially in many banks, and total losses from bad consumer debts, although each charge-off account is relatively small, often exceed the losses from all other types of loans combined. The problems that may arise from consumer loans are evidenced by the default of the Public Bank of Detroit, which was caused primarily by a low-quality portfolio of home improvement loans. In this particular case, overdue loans were rewritten with a six-month grace period in an attempt to "reduce" the amount of delinquent loans.

Consumer loans can be selected for evaluation through statistical sampling of the entire consumer loan portfolio or by using the linear programming model presented in Chapter 2. But even if a sample of several hundred consumer loans is selected from a portfolio containing thousands of accounts, it is still desirable to narrow the evaluation to the loans with the highest risk potential. For this purpose, we have derived a credit-scoring model for outstanding consumer loans.

The study presented in this chapter is different from existing credit-scoring models for consumer loans,[a] not only in applying the model to outstanding loans rather than to new loan applications, but also in attempting to develop a model that is applicable to more than one institution. The second objective is achieved by developing a combined credit-scoring model for two commercial banks and comparing this model with the individual models of each of these banks.

This chapter is a revision of an earlier paper published in the Spring 1971 issue of the *Journal of Bank Research* [53].

[a]A general discussion of credit-scoring methods appears in Chapter 3. For specific credit-scoring models for consumer loans, see, for example, Myers and Forgy [50], Apilado, Warner, and Dauten [6], and Smith [59].

The Model

The model is based on the general methodology presented in the section on "Methodology" in Chapter 3. More specifically, it is developed in a similar way to the model presented in Chapter 4, which also deals with outstanding loans. The main difference is, of course, in the definition of the variables since Chapter 4 applies to commercial rather than to consumer loans.

The dependent variable is equal to 1 for paid-up loans and 0 for charge-off accounts. Independent variables belong to three major categories:

1. Personal information on the borrower, such as monthly income, home ownership, and number of years employed by the present employer, which is listed on the original application form.
2. Subjective information provided by the loan officer, such as credit rating.
3. Loan performance data, for example, the number of overdue notices sent.

It should be noted that the second and third groups of variables can be incorporated into the analysis only because a scoring formula for outstanding rather than new consumer loans is derived. Moreover, it will be shown that these two groups contribute more to the prediction of loan quality than group 1 does. A complete list of the original independent variables from which the final elements in the formula are selected appears in Appendix 5A.

Both the selection of the variables that provide the best discrimination between good and bad loans, and the determination of their coefficients are based on multivariate regression analysis. The analysis is repeated three times to derive individual models for two commercial banks and a combined model.

Once a credit score is calculated for each loan, it is compared to two cutoff levels. Since good loans are assigned the value of 1 and bad loans the value of 0, all loans with scores above the higher cutoff level are considered to be good and are eliminated from the review process. Loans with scores below the lower cutoff level are considered to be potentially bad and are subjected to a detailed evaluation. Loans with intermediate scores are reviewed briefly by a loan review officer or a bank examiner and classified into one of the other two categories.

Because of the difficulties in obtaining the necessary cost information, as well as other parameters, for the optimal derivation of the cutoff levels, we use the same decision rule that has been used in Chapter 4. Namely, the proportion of actually bad loans wrongly classified as good should be less than 5 percent of all bad loans and the proportion of bad loans classified correctly as bad should be at least 75 percent of total bad loans (the remainder falls into the marginal category). The emphasis on bad loans is explained by the relatively high cost of overlooking a potentially bad loan compared with the cost of evaluating a good loan (in practice, some rough cost estimates should be used in determining the appropriate decision rule). Given this decision rule, the cutoff levels are determined by trial and error based on the original sample observations. The cutoff levels together with the scoring function are then tested on the holdout sample.

The Data

The data were collected from two commercial banks. All loans that were charged-off during a predetermined period were included in the study and matched with randomly selected good loans. The matching was based on the type of loan—for example, automobile, medical, travel, education, and so on. The number of observations was close to 400 in the first bank and over 300 in the second bank, for a total of 700 in the combined model. From these observations, fifty pairs of bad and good accounts were randomly selected for each bank (100 pairs for the combined case) to serve as a holdout sample for testing the models' results.

Since the data were obtained from two different commercial banks that use different application forms and, more important, different control techniques, there are some variations in the items incorporated into each of the three models. Obviously, the combined model includes only those elements that are available from both banks.

Empirical Results

The Credit-Scoring Function

The credit-scoring functions of all three models are presented in Table 5-1. The first variable (x_1) measures the applicant's employment stability and the second variable (x_2) indicates whether or not he has a checking account. Since the dependent variable is equal to 1 for good loans and 0 for bad accounts, the positive coefficients show, as expected, that a longer employment period and ownership of a checking account are associated with better credit risks. The third variable (x_3) relates to the present living accommodations of the borrower but is defined somewhat differently in each of the three models: in the first bank, it indicates whether the borrower rents or not; in the second bank, it indicates whether or not the borrower pays a mortgage; and in the combined model, it measures the monthly mortgage payment (in dollars). A negative coefficient for Model 1 (renting) and two positive coefficients for Models 2 and 3 consistently indicate that homeowners are better credit risks than renters. Similarly, car owners (x_4) are better risks than borrowers who do not own an automobile.

Unlike the first four variables, for which information can be obtained directly from the application form, variables 5 and 6 are based on the judgment of a loan officer. Variable 5 combines the available information about the customer's credit record, such as payment performance on other loans and credit references. While such a combined variable can be formulated as a weighted index of several items, in this case, it was subjectively derived by a loan officer who assigned to each loan one of three possible values: high (1), average (2), or low (3). Since the lowest value corresponds to the highest credit rating, a negative coefficient correctly indicates that a better credit rating is associated with good loans. Variable 6, which was available only in one bank (Model 2), is somewhat similar. In this bank, an applicant with a marginal credit record is required to open a joint loan account with his (or her) spouse. As expected, a negative coefficient indicates that a joint account is more risky than a loan with a single signature.

The last two variables measure the loan's payment history in terms of the number of overdue notices (x_7) and number of early

Table 5-1
Regression Results: The Three Credit-Scoring Functions
Coefficients and Standard Errors (in parentheses)[a]

Variable (x_i)	Model 1	Model 2	Model 3 (combined)
1. Years with present employer	0.0092 (0.0038)	0.0068 (0.0034)	0.0130 (0.0032)
2. Owns checking account (yes-no)	0.1129 (0.0516)	0.1134 (0.0546)	0.2183 (0.0465)
3. Mortgage (rent)	−0.1241 (0.0481)	0.1527 (0.0706)	0.0009 (0.0004)
4. Owns automobile (yes-no)	...[b]	0.1839 (0.0542)	...[b]
5. Credit (high-average-low)	−0.0831 (0.0352)	...[b]	−0.1410 (0.0299)
6. Type of account (joint-other)	...[c]	−0.6490 (0.0570)	...[c]
7. Overdue notices (number)	−0.0388 (0.0076)	...[c]	...[c]
8. Over/under (months)	0.0852 (0.0120)	...[c]	...[c]
Intercept	0.7860	0.5090	0.5733
R^2	0.4219	0.5960	0.1838

[a]All listed variables are significant at the 5 percent level or better.
[b]Insignificant at 5 percent level.
[c]Data not available.

(over: positive) or late (under: negative) payments (x_8). This information was readily available for only one of the banks (Model 1), which uses a computer in managing its consumer loan portfolio. Not surprisingly, the negative coefficient of x_7 shows that, as the number of overdue notices increases, the chances of payoff are smaller. Likewise, the positive coefficient of x_8 indicates that early payments, as opposed to late payments, are associated with better credit risks.

It was expected that variables belonging to group 3 (performance data) and group 2 (subjective evaluation) contribute more to the prediction of the dependent variable (loan quality) than variables belonging to group 1 (personal information). This assumption has been confirmed both by more significant coefficients, as can be seen in Table 5-1, and in terms of contribution to R^2, that is, explanation of the variance of the dependent variable. The second confirmation was obtained from a variable deletion routine and from a stepwise regression program. For example, if we delete variables 7 and 8 from Model 1, R^2 is reduced from 0.422 to 0.194. Eliminating variables 5, 7, and 8 results in $R^2 = 0.139$. It is not surprising, therefore, that these variables enter first into a forward stepwise regression program. Table 5-2 represents the results of the stepwise program for Model 1. Similar results are obtained for Models 2 and 3 where variables 6 and 5, respectively, provide the largest contributions to R^2.

Loan Classifications

The reclassifications of the observations from the original sample are presented in Table 5-3. These results are obtained by using the cutoff levels that were defined according to the decision rule specified earlier in this chapter in the section on "The Model." Since this rule emphasizes the correct classification of bad debts, the classification results for this category are much better than the ones obtained for good loans. In the first model, for example, 76.8 percent of loans that are actually bad are correctly classified, compared to 52.0 percent for good loans. The classification results obtained from the third model for loans that are actually good are even worse; only 30.5 percent are correctly classified as good. This result is not surprising since the combined model does not include some of the best discriminatory variables (numbers 6, 7, and 8) contained in the individual models (see Tables 5-1 and 5-2). The classifications in the third model of loans that are actually bad are, of course, within the limits specified by the decision rule.

As explained in Chapter 3, the reclassification of the original observations are biased because the models are derived from the same data. Hence, the models are tested by using the holdout samples (see Table 5-4). Compared with the reclassifications of the original samples, the results for the holdout samples are somewhat better for actually good loans (in all three models), and somewhat less accurate for actually bad loans (in Models 1 and 2), but the differences are relatively small. Nevertheless, the classifications of actually bad loans in the first two models violate slightly the specifications of the decision rule for selecting the cutoff levels. Since the

Table 5-2
Contributions of the Independent Variables to R^2—Model 1

Step	Variable	R^2	Increase in R^2
1	Over/under (8)	0.274	0.274
2	Overdue notices (7)	0.345	0.071
3	Credit (5)	0.380	0.035
4	Mortgage (3)	0.401	0.021
5	Years with present employer (1)	0.412	0.011
6	Owns checking account (2)	0.422	0.010

Table 5-3
Classification Results—Original Samples (in Percentages)

		Predicted			
	Actual	Good	Marginal	Bad	Total
Model 1	Bad	4.8	18.4	76.8	100.0
	Good	52.0	36.3	11.7	100.0
Model 2	Bad	3.6	20.5	75.9	100.0
	Good	58.8	33.3	7.9	100.0
Model 3	Bad	4.8	17.8	77.4	100.0
	Good	30.5	35.3	34.2	100.0

Table 5-4
Classification Results—Holdout Samples (in Percentages)

		Predicted			
	Actual	Good	Marginal	Bad	Total
Model 1	Bad	4.0	30.0	66.0	100.0
	Good	60.0	36.0	4.0	100.0
Model 2	Bad	6.0	24.0	70.0	100.0
	Good	60.0	38.0	2.0	100.0
Model 3	Bad	3.0	16.0	81.0	100.0
	Good	40.0	31.0	29.0	100.0

decision rule was determined arbitrarily, these differences do not seem to justify a revision of the model. However, in actual implementations of the model, when certain cost information is available, variations should be examined carefully to determine whether they justify a revision of the model.

In addition to comparing the classification results of the original and holdout samples, we also compared the results with conventional consumer loan review methods. Classifications based on various conventional decision rules have been compared with the models' results, and in all cases the models provided better classifications. One rule of thumb that was checked for bank 1, for instance, classified loans as bad if they were either three months or longer overdue or received more than three late payment notices. Accounts that were either one or two months overdue or received two or three late payment notices were classified as marginal. All other loans were classified as good. The classifications of the holdout sample of bank 1 based on this rule are presented in Table 5-5. It is obvious that these results are inferior to the ones obtained from Model 1 (see Table 5-4) for bad loans and better for good loans. But since the purpose of the model is to identify poor credit risks, the model is clearly superior to the conventional decision rule. Similar results were obtained in other comparisons with conventional practices.

Concluding Comments

This chapter contains three credit-scoring models for outstanding consumer loans. Two of the models apply to each of two individual banks, and the third one is a combined model that applies to both banks. The first two models are of interest to loan review officers in these institutions. Their usefulness depends, of course, on the cost of operating the model and on its effect on the review process. Since the derivation and implementation of a credit-scoring model for existing consumer loans is quite simple, and since the model is likely to reduce substantially the work load of loan review officers, it is assumed that a model of this type is applicable to most banking institutions with sizable consumer loan portfolios.

The third model is of special interest to examiners of bank regulatory agencies. Normally, bank examiners do not evaluate

Table 5-5
**Classification Results Based on a Rule of Thumb; Bank 1—Holdout
Sample (in percentages)**

Actual	Prediction			Total
	Good	Marginal	Bad	
Bad	30.0	28.0	42.0	100.0
Good	92.0	6.0	2.0	100.0

individual consumer loans except for listing delinquent accounts as substandard, doubtful, or loss, depending on the number of missing payments and on other performance data. It is obvious that a credit-scoring model could be very useful for bank examination purposes. However, it is impractical for bank examiners to derive individual credit-scoring models for each banking institution. For examination purposes, a general credit-scoring model could be the answer to this problem.

Unfortunately, the combined model presented in this chapter is inferior to the individual models. Moreover, since this model applies to only two banks, a more general model is likely to be even less efficient. Nevertheless, the classification results for the holdout sample are encouraging enough to suggest that additional research be done on general purpose credit-scoring models. The key to the success of such research is the identification of discriminatory variables for which information is easily available. Because of cross-section differences, it is highly unlikely that a single model would be applicable to all banks. A more promising prospect is to develop regional models for groups of similar banks in each region.

Appendix 5A:
Input Variables

Description	Unit	Comments
1. Home address	0, 1	poverty area = 0; other = 1
2. Years there	years	
3. Years at previous address	years	
4. Sex	0, 1	female = 1; male = 0
5. Age	years	
6. Marital Status	00, 01, 10	single = 10; married = 01; other = 00
7. Home phone	0, 1	yes = 1; no = 0
8. Monthly rent	in dollars	
9. Dependents	number	
10. Years with present employer	years	
11. Salary (annual)	in dollars	
12. Other income (annual)	in dollars	
13. Years with previous employer	years	
14. Spouse: age	years	
15. Spouse: salary (annual)	in dollars	
16. Checking account	0, 1	yes = 1: no = 0
17. Savings account	0, 1	yes = 1; no = 0
18. Bank Customer	0, 1	yes = 1; no = 0
19. Monthly mortgage	in dollars	
20. Present automobile; year	. . .	two digits
21. Credit rating	1, 2, 3	high = 1; average = 2; low = 3
22. Type of account	0, 1	joint = 1; other = 0
23. Personal income (annual)	in dollars	variables 11 + 12
24. Family income (annual)	in dollars	variables 23 + 15
25. Auto	0, 1	yes = 1; no = 0 (based on variable 20)
26. Rent	0, 1	yes = 1; no = 0 (based on variable 8)
27. Mortgage	0, 1	yes = 1; no = 0 (based on variable 19)
28. Overdue notices	number	
29. Over/under	± months	early (over: positive) or late (under: negative) payments
30. Loan quality (dependent variable)	0, 1	good = 1; bad = 0

6

Estimating Losses from a Consumer Loans Portfolio: A Markov Chains Approach

This chapter presents a complex problem that was faced by a Federal bank regulatory agency (the FDIC) and solved with advanced analytical methods. The problem concerned the estimation of potential losses from a large consumer loans portfolio (20,000 accounts amounting to $17 million) held by a closed commercial bank. This estimate, which was requested by the court, represents the amount the FDIC, as receiver, offered the commercial bank that acquired this portfolio (the assuming bank). After two depositions concerning the estimate, the two parties (FDIC and the assuming bank) reached a settlement that was quite close to the estimated amount.

Although the estimation method described in this chapter was designed for a specific case, it may be applicable, with some modifications, to similar situations—that is, when the potential loss from an entire consumer loans portfolio must be estimated for acquisition, investment, or special examination purposes. For routine reviews and examinations, this method is too complex and is therefore economically unjustified.

The Problem

In October 1966, a large commercial bank failed. A major portion of the defaulted bank's assets was held in consumer credit. As of the closing date (12 October 1966), the loan portfolio contained over 38,000 consumer loans that amounted to more than $43 million. Most of these loans were unsecured home improvement loans (with five- to seven-years' maturity) owned by residents in urban poverty areas. The poor quality of these loans was considered to be the main cause for the bank's failure.

Following the bank's default, its receiver (the FDIC) arranged a takeover by another commercial bank in the same area. Because of

This chapter is an extension of an earlier paper published in B. Avi Itzhak (ed.) *Developments in Operations Research* [54].

the poor quality of the loan portfolio, the FDIC agreed to assume any loan that became delinquent over 180 days. To avoid a long collection effort, however, the FDIC decided to continue this arrangement for only eighteen months after the closing day, that is, up to 12 April 1968 (the settlement date). In turn, the FDIC agreed to pay the acquiring bank a lump sum for the total estimated losses on the remaining loan portfolio as of the settlement date. The specific terms of the receiver's sale agreement, between the FDIC and the assuming bank, stipulated that "the gross purchase price (paid by the assuming bank) shall be decreased on the settlement date by estimating unrealized losses mutually agreed upon by the parties on all loans purchased at a value not to exceed the figure at which the assuming bank acquired it."

While commercial loans had been analyzed individually to determine their potential loss after the settlement date, this approach could not be applied to consumer loans for several reasons. First, as of 12 April 1968, the portfolio included almost 20,000 consumer loans, amounting to $17 million, in fifty-four different categories. Second, the information on the loan applications was at least three years old. Finally, the loss experience from the portfolio was much higher than normal losses from similar loan types. Despite these difficulties, it was necessary to obtain the best possible estimate of potential losses from these consumer loans.

Alternative Approaches

Three different approaches could have been used to solve the loss estimation problem. First, average loss ratios could have been applied to each loan category. Second, each loan could have been evaluated individually, either with a credit-scoring model or by a bank examiner. Finally, past performance of the portfolio could have been projected into the future.

Although average loss percentages for each type of loan in every state are compiled by the ABA Installment Credit Committee, these ratios could not have been used in this case since the quality of the portfolio was much lower than a normal consumer loans portfolio. The evaluation of individual loans by bank examiners was also impossible, not because of the portfolio's size (a sample could have

FORM 16-0001 (10/74)

* 1-OP - OUT OF PRINT - CANNOT SUPPLY
3-NYP - NOT YET PUBLISHED - WILL SHIP WHEN READY
4-OS - OUT OF STOCK - BACK ORDERED UNLESS OTHERWISE INSTRUCTED

PICKED BY	CHECKED BY	PACKED BY	NO. OF CTNS.	WEIGHT
22	CC	# 4	1	

DATE SHIPPED	PARCEL POST	EXPRESS	C.O.D.
7-9-75			

Jul 9 9 32 AM '75

been taken), but simply because it is extremely difficult to determine whether an outstanding unsecured consumer loan will eventually end up as a loss. Similarly, a credit-scoring model that would be very useful for routine reviews and examinations of existing loans would, in this case, be inapplicable to the problem. As shown in previous chapters, the credit-scoring model points out the riskier accounts for further evaluation and closer control. It does not provide an estimate of expected losses from these loans, although a loan classification is a good *ex ante* indicator of some future losses, either partial or complete.

This left the third approach as the best way to solve the estimation problem. Here, again, there were a number of methods that could have been used. One could have been based on a straightforward projection of past performance of the entire portfolio into the future. This solution was rejected because the payment behavior had changed substantially since the closing date. Another alternative was to obtain loss predictions from a time-series analysis. This approach was attempted but rejected because of missing data and primarily because of the substantial differences in the payment performance of current and delinquent loans. Moreover, current and delinquent loans were strongly related through frequent transitions from one status to the other and among different delinquency states.

The method used for projecting the past performance of the portfolio into the future is based on a Markov chains process. This method enables one to predict the future status of a system that is undergoing frequent transitions among a number of states.[a] In essence, the liquidation process of a consumer loans portfolio can be represented by an absorbing Markov chain since each loan in the portfolio eventually has to be either paid-up or charged-off. Moreover, Cyert, Davidson, and Thompson (CDT) [18] have shown that Markov chains can be used by retail establishments to estimate their reserves for bad debts on consumer accounts. Since they have developed and proved the necessary mathematical theorems for solving this problem, their method will be used, subject to certain modifications required by the special characteristics of this case.

---

[a]An illustration of the Markov chains process is provided in Appendix 6A for the reader who is not familiar with this process.

The Data

Although the total portfolio was divided into fifty-four types of loans, most accounts were concentrated in nine categories of home improvement loans. On 28 October 1966, 76.1 percent of the dollar volume was included in these nine types. This ratio increased to 89.1 percent by 12 April 1968, and 94.1 percent by 28 November 1968. Moreover, 97.7 percent of the dollar volume of delinquent loans on 12 April 1968 was from these nine types (see Appendix 6B). Another indicator of the riskiness of these categories is the ratio of delinquent loans to total loans, which was 13.8 percent for the nine categories, compared to 2.7 percent for all other loans. For these reasons, it was decided to concentrate on the nine loan categories and to treat all other types of accounts as regular consumer loans with normal delinquency and loss ratios.

A sample of 1000 accounts was randomly selected from the nine types according to the share of these loan categories in the outstanding balance of the entire portfolio. For example, if the total balance of a certain category was 20 percent of the overall total, 200 loans were selected from this category. This procedure was followed because of differences in the average size of loans in some of these categories. Nevertheless, since all nine categories included home improvement loans with similar characteristics except for size, the 1000 accounts were treated as a single sample representing a single population of the nine loan categories. The statistical validity of the sample was examined through chi-square tests by comparing the actual and expected distributions of loans into the various delinquency states. These tests indicate that the sample provides a statistically valid representation of the population.[b]

Three consecutive transition matrices were derived by determining the delinquency status of each sample loan on four dates eight to nine months apart[c]: 28 October 1966, 23 June 1967, 23 February 1968, and 28 November 1968. The reason for obtaining three ma-

---

[b]The results of one chi-square test (for 23 February 1968), which are significant at the 5 percent level, are presented in Appendix 6C.

[c]The use of long intervals avoided seasonal and other short-run fluctuations in the payment performance, which were irrelevant and misleading for the long-run liquidation projection. Note that the last date (28 November 1968) is beyond the settlement date (12 April 1968). This is because the computation was performed only at the end of 1968 and all the available data at that time had been utilized. The specific dates of observations were determined by data availability.

trices rather than one was to check, by comparing the entries of these matrices, whether the Markov process was stationary. On each of the four dates, a loan could have been in only one of six states:

1. Current (up to twenty-nine days late).
2. From thirty to fifty-nine days delinquent.
3. From sixty to 119 days delinquent.
4. Over 120 days delinquent.
5. Repaid.
6. Loss.

As of October 1966, the random sample included 849 current loans, sixty-five loans delinquent thirty to fifty-nine days, fifty-two loans delinquent sixty to 119 days, and thirty-four loans delinquent 120 days or longer. There were obviously no loans in the repaid or loss states. On the next date (23 June 1967), eighty-eight of the original 1000 loans in the sample were paid up and forty-four were charged-off as losses. The remaining 868 loans either changed their delinquency status or remained in the same state. (A transition matrix that provides a detailed description of these changes is presented in Appendix 6D.)

On 23 June 1967, the portfolio contained only 868 current and delinquent loans belonging to the original sample. The status of each of these loans was determined as of 23 February 1968, resulting in a transition matrix for that period (see Appendix 6E). Another matrix was obtained by tracing the remaining 715 loans (as of 23 February 1968) on 28 November 1968 (see Appendix 6F). These empirically derived transition matrices describe the performance of the consumer loans portfolio, as represented by the sample, over a twenty-five-month period and provide the necessary data for the Markov chains analysis.

The Solution

An examination of Appendices 6D, 6E, and 6F indicates immediately that the three empirically derived matrices are different from one another. This means that the loan liquidation process was not stationary. At this point, we could have either abandoned the

Markov chains approach or tried to solve a nonstationary process. The first choice was unacceptable since all other alternative solutions were rejected, and an estimate had to be made. On the other hand, the mathematical complexity of the second approach was prohibitive and the applicability of this approach to our specific problem was questionable.

To obtain a solution, a third method was chosen. Each transition matrix was treated as representing a stationary Markov process and its loss vector was derived. Each of these vectors represented the absorption probabilities in the loss state, assuming that the same transition matrix would be valid until the entire portfolio was liquidated. For example, when the matrix appearing in Appendix 6D was used, the assumption was that the payment behavior would continue in exactly the same manner as it did between October 1966 and June 1967 until all the loans are either paid-up or charged-off. The same applied to the other two matrices and their loss vectors.

Given this assumption, and by following the CDT approach, we compiled a matrix of absorption probabilities for each transition matrix (see Cyert, Davidson, and Thompson [18])[d]: $NR = (I - Q)^{-1}R$, where N is the fundamental matrix of the absorbing Markov chain, R is a 4×2 matrix, and Q is a 4×4 matrix, both contained in the transition matrix P. Since the sum of absorption probabilities for each row is 1, we were only interested in the loss column—that is, the vector containing the loss probabilities for each of the four original states. (The three loss vectors are presented in Table 6-1).

The differences among the three vectors agree with our observation about variations among the transition matrices. It is interesting to note, however, that the loss probabilities follow a clear trend from vector 1 to vector 3. The trend declines sharply for the first two states and rises slightly for the last two states. For instance, the loss probability of current loans declines from 0.353 in vector 1 to 0.170 in vector 3. This means that, if the payment performance continued as it did between October 1966 and June 1967, the loss percentage from current loans would have been more than twice the loss probability based on the payment performance between February and November 1968.

Given these empirical observations, the decision was to perform a trend adjustment on the loss probabilities of each state. Although

---

[d]This specific approach is relevant in our case since there were no additions to the original portfolio, which was gradually liquidated.

Table 6-1
Loss Vectors for Current and Delinquent Loans

Original state	(1) October 1966 to June 1967	(2) June 1967 to February 1968	(3) February 1968 to November 1968
Current	0.353	0.294	0.170
30-59 days delinquent	0.624	0.534	0.311
60-119 days delinquent	0.731	0.738	0.790
Over 120 days delinquent	0.894	0.963	0.991

this approach is contradictory to the underlying assumptions of the Markov process, it did provide an empirically justified solution to the difficult estimation problem. Moreover, the loss probabilities of an additional vector, which was later computed, continued along the same trend lines and confirmed the validity of our approach.

There is also a behavioral justification to the trend in the expected loss probabilities. During the first period following the bank's closing, the transition of accounts into delinquency was the highest. As the borrowers became aware of the takeover, and the collection effort by the assuming bank continued, the payment performance improved. Moreover, accounts that remained current more than eighteen months after the closing date were much more likely to have payments continued. This explanation applies to current loans and accounts with a relatively short delinquency period. On the other hand, loans delinquent over sixty days were more likely to default under any circumstances.

The trend adjustment for current loans, based on the entries in Table 6-1, is presented in Figure 6-1, where the loss probabilities apply to the beginning of each time interval. It shows that the slope between June 1967 and February 1968 was even steeper than the one between October 1966 and June 1967; hence, it can be safely assumed that the downward trend beyond February would continue at least at the same rate, resulting in a 14.7 percent loss figure for 12 April 1968 (the settlement date). It is also assumed that the loss figure would eventually become stable at 0.6 percent. This figure represents the average gross loss ratio on home improvement loans.[e]

[e]The five-year average (1963-1967) of gross losses on home modernization loans was 0.58 percent, or approximately 0.6 percent, of outstanding balances, based on the 1967 Installment Credit Survey [35, pp. 14-17].

The average of 0.6 percent and 14.7 percent (the 12 April figure) is 7.65 percent and represents, given the assumptions, the estimate of expected losses from current loans. Namely, the appropriate loss ratio is 7.65 percent and not 14.7 percent because it is assumed that the loss proportion will continue to decline along the same slope (see Figure 6-1) until it reaches the stabilization level.

A similar downward trend adjustment was applied to loans thirty to fifty-nine days delinquent, with the exception of the stabilization rate, which was assumed to equal 1 percent.[f] The results of this adjustment are presented in Table 6-2, together with the upward trend extension of loans that were sixty to 119 days delinquent. A 90 percent stabilization rate was arbitrarily defined for these loans since it was unlikely that the charge-off rate would be higher. The last state (loans overdue more than 120 days) steadily approached a 100 percent loss but was not included in the trend adjustment since the FDIC decided to accept all loans that were over 120 days delinquent on 12 April 1968.

The outcome of the trend adjustment is a single loss vector (number 4 in Table 6-2) that applies to the loan portfolio as of the settlement date. However, part or all of the accounts that would eventually be charged-off as losses, particularly the current ones, receive at least a number of payments prior to charge-off. Therefore, the expected loss in terms of dollars is less than the percentages given in vector 4, owing to the necessary adjustments for partial payments. This and other adjustments are required in this case since they have a substantial impact on the final loss estimate.

Adjustments

The adjustment for partial payments was based on the difference between the balance on 28 October 1966, and the charge-off balance of all the loans in the sample that resulted in a loss after that date. For example, a loan with a $1000 balance on 28 October 1966, and a $900 balance on the day of charge-off—say, 15 September 1967—had a

---

[f]Based on the loss percentages in vector 3 (Table 6-1) and for 12 April 1968, loss from loans thirty to fifty-nine days delinquent is approximately 80 percent higher than the loss from current loans. It is assumed, therefore, that the stabilization level for loans thirty to fifty-nine days delinquent will be 80 percent higher than the one for current loans, that is, about 1 percent.

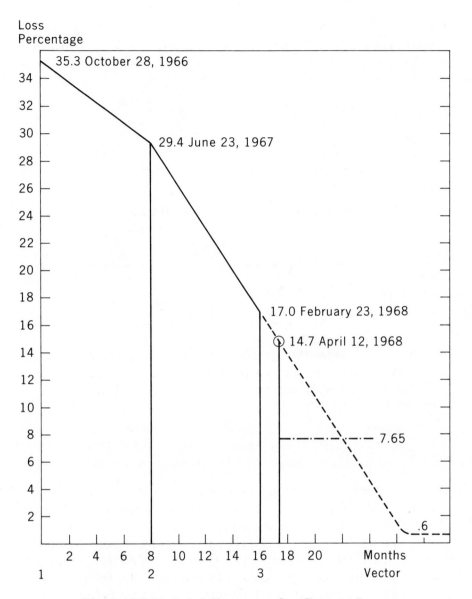

Loss
Percentage

Figure 6-1. Trend Adjustment for Current Loans

partial payment of $100, or 10 percent of the original balance. This
calculation was performed for the 157 sample loans that became a

Table 6-2
Trend-Adjusted Loss Vectors (in Percentages)

State	February 1968 to November 1968	12 April 1968	Level of stabilization	Average loss (vector 4)
Current	17.0	14.7	0.6	7.7
30-59 days delinquent	31.1	27.0	1.0	14.0
60-119 days delinquent	79.0	80.0	90.0	85.0

Table 6-3
Partial Payments Adjustments on Charge-Off Loans

Original state	Original balance	Charge-off balance	Difference	Ratio
Current	$135,830	$115,602	$20,228	0.149
30-59 days delinquent	78,387	71,757	6,630	0.085
60-119 days delinquent	67,181	63,586	3,595	0.054

loss between October 1966 and November 1968. As shown in Table 6-3, the partial payment ratio was computed for each relevant state.

Using the partial payment ratios to adjust vector 4, we obtain the final loss vector:

Current: $(7.7) \cdot (1-0.149) = 6.5.$

Thirty to fifty-nine days delinquent: $(14.0) \cdot (1-0.085) = 12.8.$

Sixty to 119 days delinquent $(85.0) \cdot (1-0.054) = 80.4.$

The final loss vector is applied to the balance of the consumer loans portfolio as of the settlement date to obtain the basic loss estimate.[g] (The results are presented in Table 6-4).

As specified in the receiver's sale agreement, the basic loss amount was further reduced by unearned interest on the charged-off balance, resulting in a gross loss estimate. Finally, the gross estimate was reduced by expected collections on charge-off accounts to obtain a net loss estimate.

---

[g]The total basic loss estimate in Table 6-4 applies only to the nine loan types from which the sample has been selected. The expected loss from all other types of loans was obtained by applying the same loss percentages to delinquent loans and 1.25 percent to current loans (0.5 percent per annum on a four-year declining balance). Total expected losses from all other consumer loan categories amounted to $37,039.

Table 6-4
Basic Loss Estimate in Liquidation of the Consumer Loans Portfolio

State	Loss percentage	Balance	Loss amount
Current	6.5	$12,981,188	$843,777
30-59 days delinquent	12.8	1,079,486	138,174
60-119 days delinquent	80.4	698,163	561,323
Total		$14,758,837	$1,543,274

Concluding Comments

The method used in this study to predict the liquidation of a consumer loans portfolio is somewhat unorthodox, but is was necessitated by the complexity of a practical problem and the need to obtain an explicit loss estimate. The trend adjustment to a nonstationary Markov process, which is the core of this approach, was empirically justified, since the loss probabilities of an additional loss vector, which was computed later, continued along the projected trend lines. Other estimates, like the stabilization rates, were based on the best available data but were relatively unimportant because of their minor impact on the final results. For these reasons, the resulting loss estimate was considered to be the best possible solution to the liquidation problem. It was adopted by the FDIC after a number of attempts to obtain an estimate in other ways failed to yield satisfactory results.

The effort invested in deriving the loss estimate was well-justified by the actual outcome of the case. After two depositions, the FDIC and the assuming bank reached a settlement that was quite close to the estimate. In contrast, the settlement amount was less than 50 percent of the assuming bank's original estimate, which was based on a straightforward projection of the portfolio's loss percentage between October 1966 and April 1968.

Although the method discussed here was designed for a special case, it could be used, subject to the necessary modifications, for other similar situations. For example, it could be used for examining the consumer loans portfolio of problem banks if a major portion of the assets is invested in this type of loan. It could also be used by investors who are considering the purchase of a financial institution that specializes in consumer lending. On the other hand, it is economically unjustifiable for routine reviews and examinations, which should be based on the credit-scoring models presented earlier.

Appendix 6A:
An Illustration of a Markov
Chains Process

The Markov chains process can best be explained by a simple illustration. Suppose that 80 percent of the sons of college-educated men also receive college degress, while 20 percent obtain a high school education. On the other hand, assume that the similar ratio for sons of high-school-educated men is 50 percent college (C) and 50 percent high school (HS). This relationship can be summarized in a single table or *transition matrix*:

$$
\begin{array}{cc}
 & Son \\
\end{array}
$$

$$
\begin{array}{ccc}
Father & C & HS \\
C & \begin{bmatrix} 0.80 & 0.20 \\ HS \end{bmatrix} & \begin{bmatrix} & \\ 0.50 & 0.50 \end{bmatrix}
\end{array}.
$$

Suppose now that the same relationship exists between the second and third generations. In this case, the transition between grandfathers and grandsons can be easily computed by multiplying the above transition matrix by itself:

$$
\begin{array}{cc}
 & \begin{array}{cc} C & HS \end{array} \\
\begin{array}{c} C \\ HS \end{array} & \begin{bmatrix} 0.80 & 0.20 \\ 0.50 & 0.50 \end{bmatrix}
\end{array}
\cdot
\begin{array}{cc}
 & \begin{array}{cc} C & HS \end{array} \\
 & \begin{bmatrix} 0.80 & 0.20 \\ 0.50 & 0.50 \end{bmatrix}
\end{array}
=
\begin{array}{cc}
 & \begin{array}{cc} C & HS \end{array} \\
\begin{array}{c} C \\ HS \end{array} & \begin{bmatrix} 0.74 & 0.26 \\ 0.65 & 0.35 \end{bmatrix}
\end{array}.
$$

The resulting matrix shows, for example, that 74 percent of the grandsons of college-educated men will also go to college. This figure can be easily explained: 80 percent of the sons of college-educated men will attend college, and 80 percent of their sons will also go to college, for a total of 64 percent. On the other hand, the sons of one-half of the 20 percent fraction that does not continue beyond high school will go to college, for a total of 10 percent and an overall total of 74 percent. If the transition matrix is stable, this process can continue for several more generations, where each generation is one link in a Markov chain that has two states—college and high school education. The process will finally reach an equilibrium point when the education level will be independent of the first generation.

A somewhat different Markov chain applies to a process where, eventually, all the observations concentrate in one or more absorbing states. This situation arises, for example, in the liquidation of a given portfolio of loans where each loan has to be either paid-up or charged-off. Consider a chain in which, over a one-year period, 50 percent of the current loans remain current, 20 percent become delinquent, 30 percent are paid, and none are charged-off. The same ratios for delinquent loans are: 30 percent become current, 10 percent remain delinquent, 50 percent are paid, and 10 percent are charged-off as a loss:

	Current	Delinquent	Paid	Loss
Current	0.50	0.20	0.30	0.00
Delinquent	0.30	0.10	0.50	0.10

If new loans are not added to the portfolio and the matrix is multiplied by itself several times, the final link to this Markov chain is:

	Current	Delinquent	Paid	Loss
Current	0	0	0.95	0.05
Delinquent	0	0	0.87	0.13

The results indicate that 95 percent of the current loans will eventually be paid-off and 5 percent will be charged-off, while the corresponding percentages for delinquent loans are 87 and 13, respectively.

**Appendix 6B:
Distribution of Delinquent
Loans as of 12 April 1968
(Balance in Dollars)**

Days Delinquent	Nine major types		All other types		Total	
	Number	Balance	Number	Balance	Number	Balance
30-59	1,103	$ 1,079,486	51	$ 35,202	1,154	$ 1,114,688
60-119	715	698,163	18	12,398	733	710,561
Over 120	318	296,744	4	1,962	322	298,706
Total delinquent	2,136	2,074,393	73	49,562	2,209	2,123,955
Percent delinquent	96.7	97.7	3.3	2.3	100	100
Current	14,350	12,981,188	2,730	1,799,716	17,080	14,780,904
Percent current	84.0	87.8	16.0	12.2	100	100
Total	16,486	15,055,581	2,803	1,849,278	19,289	16,904,859
Percent	85.5	89.1	14.5	10.9	100	100

**Appendix 6C:
Chi-Square Test for
Sample's Goodness of Fit,
Delinquency Status as of
23 February 1968**

Days delinquent	Distribution of entire population (percentage)	Sample (Number)			
		Actual (n_i)	Expected (e_i)	$(n_i - e_i)^2$	$(n_i - e_i)^2/e_i$
Current	86.3	620	617	9	0.01
30-59	6.0	47	43	16	0.37
60-119	4.3	23	31	64	2.06
Over 120	3.4	25	24	1	0.04
Total	100.0	715	715	90	2.48[a]

Note: The expected number of loans in each state is equal to the sample size (715) multiplied by the proportion of this state in the entire consumer loans portfolio on the same day (23 February 1968). For example, the expected number of current loans is (0.863) · (715) = 617 (rounded).

[a]Significant at the 5 percent level.

**Appendix 6D:
Transitions in Delinquency
Status and Reductions,
October 1966 to June 1967**

Status as of 28 October 1966		Status as of 23 June 1967										
		Current		30-59 days		60-119 days		Over 120 days		Paid		Loss	
Days	Number	No.	Percentage	No.	Percentage	No.	Percentage	No.	Percentage	No.	Percentage	No.	Percentage
Current	849	694	81.7	40	4.7	14	1.7	14	1.7	80	9.4	7	0.8
30-59	65	18	27.7	11	16.9	8	12.3	14	21.5	5	7.7	9	13.9
60-119	52	12	23.1	3	5.8	4	7.7	19	36.5	2	3.8	12	23.1
Over 120	34	1	2.9	1	2.9	0	0	15	44.2	1	2.9	16	47.1
Total	1000	725	72.5	55	5.5	26	2.6	62	6.2	88	8.8	44	4.4

Appendix 6E:
Transitions in Delinquency
Status and Reductions,
June 1967 to February 1968

Status as of 23 June 1967		Status as of 23 February 1968										
		Current		30-59 days		60-119 days		Over 120 days		Paid		Loss	
Days	Number	No.	Percentage	No.	Percentage	No.	Percentage	No.	Percentage	No.	Percentage	No.	Percentage
Current	725	594	81.9	32	4.4	9	1.2	5	.7	75	10.4	10	1.4
30-59	55	21	38.2	9	16.4	9	16.4	7	12.7	4	7.2	5	9.1
60-119	26	4	15.4	6	23.1	4	15.4	4	15.4	0	0	8	30.7
Over 120	62	1	1.6	0	0	1	1.6	9	14.5	1	1.6	50	80.7
Total	868	620	71.4	47	5.4	23	2.7	25	2.9	80	9.2	73	8.4

**Appendix 6F:
Transitions in Delinquency
Status and Reductions,
February 1968 to November
1968**

Status as of 23 February 1968		Status as of 28 November 1968											
		Current		30-59 days		60-119 days		Over 120 days		Paid		Loss	
Days	Number	No.	Percentage	No.	Percentage	No.	Percentage	No.	Percentage	No.	Percentage	No.	Percentage
Current	620	491	79.2	27	4.3	11	1.8	3	0.5	86	13.9	2	0.3
30-59	47	22	46.8	5	10.6	8	17.0	0	0	9	19.2	3	6.4
60-119	23	3	13.0	1	4.4	3	13.0	3	13.0	1	4.4	12	52.2
Over 120	25	0	0	0	0	1	4.0	1	4.0	0	0	23	92.0
Total	715	516	72.2	33	4.6	23	3.2	7	1.0	96	13.4	40	5.6

References

1. Abate, R. P. "Numerical Scoring Systems for Commercial Loans," *Bankers Monthly* (January 1969), pp. 38-39ff.

2. Abdel-Khalik, A. R. "Detailing Financial Information and the Loan Decision: An Empirical Study," *Journal of Commercial Bank Lending* (April 1973), pp. 41-54.

3. Altman, E. I. "Financial Ratios, Discriminant Analysis and the Prediction of Corporate Bankruptcy," *Journal of Finance* (September 1968), pp. 589-609.

4. _____. *Corporate Bankruptcy in America*, Lexington, Mass.: Lexington Books, D. C. Heath, 1971.

5. Altman, E. I., M. Margaine, M. Schlosser, and P. Vernimmen. "Financial and Statistical Analysis for Commercial Loan Evaluation: A French Experience," *Journal of Financial and Quantitative Analysis* (March 1974), pp. 195-211.

6. Apilado, V. P., D. C. Warner, and J. J. Dauten. "Evaluative Techniques in Consumer Finance—Experimental Results and Policy Implications for Financial Institutions," *Journal of Financial and Quantitative Analysis* (March 1974), pp. 275-283.

7. *Bank Operating Statistics–1973*. Washington, D.C.: Federal Deposit Insurance Corporation, 1974.

8. Barnett, R. E. "Anatomy of a Bank Failure," *Magazine of Bank Administration* (April 1972), pp. 20-23ff.

9. Bates, T. "An Econometric Analysis of Lending to Black Businessmen," *Review of Economics and Statistics* (August 1973), pp. 272-283.

10. Benston, G. J. "Substandard Loans," *National Banking Review* (March 1967), pp. 271-281.

11. _____. "Bank Examination," *The Bulletin*, New York University, Graduate School of Business Administration, Nos. 89-90 (May 1973).

12. Boggess, W. P. "Screen-Test Your Credit Risks," *Harvard Business Review* (November-December 1967), pp. 113-122.

13. Burnham, F. W. "Loan Review: A Necessary Exercise in 20-20 Hindsight," *Journal of Commercial Bank Lending* (June 1973), pp. 13-20.

105

14. Carleton, W. T., and E. M. Lerner. "Statistical Credit Scoring of Municipal Bonds," *Journal of Money, Credit and Banking* (November 1969), pp. 750-764.

15. Cohen, K. J., T. C. Gilmore, and F. A. Singer. "Bank Procedures for Analyzing Business Loan Applications," in *Analytical Methods in Banking*, K. J. Cohen and F. S. Hammer (eds.). Homewood, Ill.: Richard D. Irwin, 1966, pp. 218-251.

16. Cohen, K. J., and F. S. Hammer (eds.). *Analytical Methods in Banking*. Homewood, Ill.: Richard D. Irwin, 1966.

17. Crosse, H. D. *Management Policies for Commercial Banks*. Englewood Cliffs, N.J.: Prentice-Hall, 1962.

18. Cyert, R. M., H. J. Davidson, and G. L. Thompson. "Estimation of the Allowance for Doubtful Accounts by Markov Chains," *Management Science* (April 1962), pp. 287-303.

19. Dunham, H. L. "A Simple Credit Rating for Small Loans," *Bankers Monthly* (June 1938), pp. 332-333ff.

20. Durand, D. D. *Risk Elements in Consumer Installment Financing*, Study No. 8. New York: National Bureau of Economic Research, 1941.

21. Edmister, R. O. "Financial Ratios and Credit Scoring for Small Business Loans," *Journal of Commercial Bank Lending* (September 1971), pp. 10-23.

22. _____. "An Empirical Test of Financial Ratio Analysis for Small Business Failure Prediction," *Journal of Financial and Quantitative Analysis* (March 1972), pp. 1477-1493.

23. Eilon, S., and T. R. Fowkes (eds.). *Applications of Management Science in Banking and Finance*. London: Gower Press, 1972.

24. Eisenbeis, R. A., and R. B. Avery. *Discriminant Analysis and Classification Procedures: Theory and Applications*. Lexington, Mass.: Lexington Books, D.C. Heath, 1972.

25. Eisenbeis, R. A., and N. B. Murphy. "Interest Rate Ceilings and Consumer Credit Rationing: A Multivariate Analysis of a Survey of Borrowers," *Southern Economic Journal* (July 1974), pp. 115-123.

26. Ettinger, R. P., and D. E. Golieb. *Credits and Collections*, 5th ed. Englewood Cliffs, N.J.: Prentice-Hall, 1962.

27. Ewert, D. C. "Trade Credit Management: Selection of Accounts Receivable Using a Statistical Model," Paper No. 236, School of Industrial Administration. Lafayette, Ind.: Purdue University, March 1969.

28. Fair, W. R. "On Credit Scoring," paper presented at TIMS International Meeting, Imperial College, London (July 1970).

29. Gilbert, E. S. "On Discrimination Using Qualitative Variables," *Journal of the American Statistical Association* (December 1968), pp. 1399-1412.

30. Hall, C. B. "An Examiner Considers a Loan Account," *RMA Bulletin* (July 1967), pp. 25-29.

31. Hammer, F. S., and Y. E. Orgler. "Developments in Credit Scoring for Commercial Loans," *Journal of Commercial Bank Lending* (July 1969), pp. 25-31.

32. Hattenhouse, G. W., and J. R. Wentworth. "Credit Analysis Model—A New Look for Credit Scoring," *Journal of Commercial Bank Lending* (December 1971), pp. 26-32.

33. Horton, J. J. "Statistical Classification of Municipal Bonds," *Journal of Bank Research* (Autumn 1970), pp. 29-40.

34. Hoskin, G. J. "Some Aids to Establishing a Grading System for Commercial Loans," *Journal of Commercial Bank Lending* (May 1968), pp. 24-33.

35. *Installment Credit Survey*. New York: Installment Credit Committee, The American Bankers Association, 1967.

36. Jacobs, D. P. *The Impact of Examination Practices upon Commercial Bank Lending Policies*, House Committee on Banking and Currency, 88th Cong., 2d Sess. Washington, D.C.: Government Printing Office, 1964.

37. Jacobsen, R. A. "A Bank Examiner's Loan Review," *Journal of Commercial Bank Lending* (May 1973), pp. 48-53.

38. Jessup, P. F. (ed.). *Innovations in Bank Management: Selected Readings*. New York: Holt, Rinehart and Winston, 1969.

39. Johnston, J. *Econometric Methods*. New York: McGraw-Hill, 1963.

40. "Keeping up with New Trends in the Field of Commercial Lending, Part 2," *Banking* (June 1974), pp. 36-38ff.

41. Lachenbruch, P. A. "An Almost Unbiased Method of Obtain-

ing Confidence Intervals for the Probability of Misclassification in Discriminant Analysis," *Biometrics* (December 1967), pp. 639-645.

42. Lachenbruch, P. A., and M. R. Mickey. "Estimation of Error Rates in Discriminant Analysis," *Technometrics* (February 1968), pp. 1-11.

43. Ladd, G. W. "Linear Probability Functions and Discriminant Functions," *Econometrica* (October 1966), pp. 873-885.

44. Lane, S. "Submarginal Credit Risk Classification," *Journal of Financial and Quantitative Analysis* (January 1972), pp. 1379-1385.

45. *Manual of Examination Policies*, Section H, rev. ed. Washington, D.C.: Federal Deposit Insurance Corporation, Division of Bank Supervision, March 1973.

46. McGrath, J. J. "Improving Credit Evaluation with a Weighted Application Blank," *Journal of Applied Psychology* (October 1960), pp. 325-328.

47. Morris, R. A. "Credit Analysis: An O.R. Approach," *RMA Bulletin* (July 1966), pp. 626-638.

48. Morrison, D. G. "On the Interpretation of Discriminant Analysis," *Journal of Marketing Research* (May 1969), pp. 156-163.

49. Myers, J. H. "Numerical Scoring Systems in Retail Credit Evaluation," *Credit World* (April 1962).

50. Myers, J. H., and E. W. Forgy. "The Development of Numerical Credit Evaluation Systems," *Journal of the American Statistical Association* (September 1963), pp. 799-806.

51. Orgler, Y. E. "Selection of Bank Loans for Evaluation: An Analytical Approach," *Journal of Finance* (March 1969), pp. 75-80.

52. _____. "A Credit-Scoring Model for Commercial Loans," *Journal of Money, Credit and Banking* (November 1970), pp. 435-445.

53. _____. "Evaluation of Consumer Loans with Credit-Scoring Models," *Journal of Bank Research* (Spring 1971), pp. 31-37.

54. _____. "Estimating Losses for Bank Installment Loans: A Markov Chains Approach," in *Developments in Operations*

Research, B. Avi-Itzhak (ed.). London: Gordon and Breach, 1971, pp. 281-292.

55. Pinches, G. E., and K. A. Mingo. "A Multivariate Analysis of Industrial Bond Ratings," *Journal of Finance* (March 1973), pp. 1-18.

56. Roberts, R. G. "Loan Take-Off Limit," *Proceedings of the Conference of Examiners and Assistant Examiners of the Tenth Federal Deposit Insurance Corporation District.* Kansas City: FDIC, November 1965.

57. Sax, S. W. "Loan Review-Bank Quality Control and R&D," *Bankers Magazine* (September 1973), pp. 72-76.

58. Searle, S. R., and J. G. Udell. "The Use of Regression on Dummy Variables in Management Research," *Management Science* (February 1970), pp. 397-409.

59. Smith, P. F. "Measuring Risk on Consumer Installment Credit," *Management Science* (November 1964), pp. 327-340.

60. Williams, S. "Survey Shows Increasing Importance of Mathematical Aids to Management," *Journal of Bank Research* (Summer 1970), pp. 6-8.

61. Wu, H. K. "Bank-Examiner Criticisms, Bank Loan Defaults, and Bank Loan Quality," *Journal of Finance* (September 1969), pp. 697-705.

62. Zaegal, R. J. "A Point Rating System for Evaluating Customers," *Credit World* (October 1963).

63. Zimmerman, C. G. "The Fourth Dimension of Credit Evaluation: Experience," *RMA Bulletin* (February 1967), pp. 15-20.

Index

Index

113

About the Author

Yair E. Orgler is a visiting professor with the Board of Governors of the Federal Reserve System. He received the Ph.D. from the Carnegie-Mellon University, Graduate School of Industrial Administration in 1967 and was a financial economist with the Division of Research at the Federal Deposit Insurance Corporation from 1967 to 1969 and from 1973 to 1974. Dr. Orgler is affiliated with the Leon Recanati Graduate School of Business Administration at Tel-Aviv University and, between 1969 and 1973, was director of research at the Israel Institute of Business Research and consultant to the Israel Examiner of Banks.